Praise for *Crea*

"Before I met Aviv, I was an e... leader. Our teams were focused on improvement, functioning well and consistently delivering strong results. I wasn't convinced that we needed help. Then, through a series of conversations, I agreed to give Aviv an opportunity to work with my senior staff. After several engagements with Aviv, our teams rapidly took performance to the breakout level. His methods helped us quickly transform our learning and insights into a coherent set of activities which created a remarkable new future, one in which we achieved many years of industry-leading performance in growth, market share, profitability and customer satisfaction. I highly recommend his book, *Create New Futures* to leaders who desire to build stronger teams and dramatically improve the trajectory of their business."

—Ted Clark, former Senior VP and GM, Hewlett-Packard

"Finally, after 12 years of Aviv's inspirational work with my teams in three different companies, *Create New Futures* is here. Like Aviv's strategy workshops, this book will make you think in entirely new ways about your business, about life, and about your life. As a result, you will be richer, stronger, and more prepared to embark on your development journey ahead."

—David Berman, President, Zoom Video Communications

"This is an engagingly honest book about the work of building an organizational future through a series of provocative questions and essential conversations. Aviv helped author what became my organizational strategy for transforming marketing strategy at P&G. In *Create New Futures,* Aviv shares his expertise to help you create momentum in your leadership work as if he were coaching you in real-time."

—Daniel Epstein, former Harley Procter Marketing Director, Procter & Gamble; Principal, Daniel Epstein & Associates, LTD.

"Your organization's future success depends on innovation. Leaders hold the key to fostering an environment where innovation flourishes. Aviv's masterful story-telling inspires, enlightens, and compels leaders to embrace actions that create a preferred future in every part of their lives. Begin to create your desired future with this powerful book."

—Elaine Biech, author, The Art and Science of Training, Editor, The ASTD Leadership Handbook

---

"Accelerating the achievement of our organizational and business objectives was the focus of Aviv's developmental work with me and my team. Our dynamic collaboration honed my leadership skills and inspired our entire team to push our performance far beyond what we had thought possible. *Create New Futures* codifies Aviv's methods and illustrates how he works with senior teams to facilitate momentous learning and produce breakthrough results. You and your team can reap significant benefits by applying Aviv's wisdom in your organization."

—Astrid Hartmann, Senior Vice President, Lufthansa Global Business

---

"In *Create New Futures*, Aviv Shahar makes a compelling case for utilizing conversations to shape one's desired future. By applying his insights and supporting steps to challenge their thinking, leaders can achieve breakthrough results."

—Jorge Mesquita, Executive Vice President, Johnson & Johnson and Worldwide Chairman, Johnson & Johnson Consumer Companies

---

"Insightful. In *Create New Futures*, Aviv shares the process he applied to help my team deliver transformational results. How do we create rapid developments? Through a series of powerful conversations to converge on a compelling vision, translated into well-articulated outcomes and a set of actionable strategies. Every leader must read this book."

—Ike Harris, Vice President, Supply Chain Cisco Systems

"*Create New Futures* is transformative. A fantastic author explains how great actions lead to breakthroughs. Aviv Shahar reminds me of the guy who's told, 'That idea is global' and replies, 'No, it's much bigger than that.' Read this book and change the world before the world changes you."
—*Alan Weiss, PhD, author,* **Million Dollar Maverick, Million Dollar Consulting,** *and over 60 other books.*

"No matter WHAT page you turn to, you are going to connect immediately with the power you possess to change your future. Through my work with Aviv, I have learned that he exhibits his innate ability to drive the right conversations for you to discover the growth and success we all truly want. I dare you to read this book and not come away with the clarity you have been looking for, and the tools to create your path."
—*Alice Latino, Co-Founder Heavenly Care Home Health, former Vice President Operations Emeritus Senior Living*

"Everyone should read *Create New Futures*! In my 25+ years management career at Hewlett-Packard, including my role as Chief Learning Officer, Aviv has been undeniably the most impactful consultant and coach I have worked with. This book integrates the practical and the inspirational elements of Aviv's work: we change organizations, and the world at large, one conversation at a time."
—*Sam Szteinbaum, Chairman & CEO at The Wonder Years, Inc; former Chief Learning Officer, Hewlett-Packard*

"See for yourself why so many large corporations rely on Aviv to help guide their future. This book is chock full of simple, useful models to help executives open new organizational portals through innovative approaches and strategic thinking. Special stories illustrate every major point. Aviv's concise questions alone can provide hours of inspired pondering."
—*Geoff Bellman, author,* **Extraordinary Groups and Getting Things Done When You Are Not in Charge**

"Practical and inspiring! *Create New Futures* delivers immediately applicable frameworks and tools for every leader. Aviv Shahar brings to life a fresh and unique approach I have experienced firsthand when he helped my team develop strategies and produce exceptional business results. His ability to pick up the conversation's essence, translate it to easily understandable language, and convert complex themes to actionable steps is amazing. This book is a game-changer."
—*V. Ravichandran, Founder CEO, Alive Consulting, ex-Senior Vice President, Global Business Services, Hewlett-Packard*

"Working with Aviv truly is a transformational experience. Applying his strategies over the years has allowed me to inspire and transform my teams, achieve balance, and focus on what matters. In his practical and thought provoking book *Create New Futures*, Aviv Shahar frames the steps you must take with your team to create your desired future and shows you how to use the art of conversation to build your next success horizons. Keep this inspiring book handy: the conversation strategies it offers have the power to enrich every aspect of your life."
—*Faiza Hughell, Vice President, Sales at RingCentral*

"I plan to give copies of *Create New Futures* to the leaders of all of the organizations I care about, and to keep it close at hand for my own inspiration and encouragement. Aviv's book empowers individuals and businesses to construct the futures they most long for by effortlessly blending personal and spiritual development with extraordinarily effective step-by-step processes. For more than a decade I have relied on Aviv's wise counsel and his masterful ability to ask questions and frame metaphors to illuminate my thinking horizons, expand my understanding of what's possible, and lead to practical epiphanies."
—*Christy Lee-Engel, ND, EAMP, founding Director of the Bastyr University Center for Mind, Body, Spirit and Nature*

"A must-read for current and aspiring leaders. In *Create New Futures* Aviv asks the hard questions, as he does in his live coaching and consulting. This book will make you think in a new and groundbreaking way about your work and about being a leader. Most importantly, Aviv connects business growth with personal growth, which is the ultimate aim of all good leaders."
—Gilad Berenstein, CEO Utrip

———————————

"What if conversations at work produced profound breakthroughs? *Create New Futures* shows how they can and offers a set of strategies to help you lead your transformation. Aviv's work enabled my team to dramatically accelerate our results. I recommend you read and apply Aviv's methods."
—Shelley Stewart, Vice President & CPO, DuPont

———————————

Create New Futures

How Leaders Produce
Breakthroughs and Transform
the World Through Conversation

Aviv Shahar

ISBN: 978-0-9815509-9-2

KORA
PRESS

Printed in the United States of America

Create New Futures

*How Leaders Produce
Breakthroughs and Transform
the World Through Conversation*

Aviv Shahar

Dedication

To Sara my wife and to Edan our son,
I continue to learn from you. Thank you.

To Zvi my father and Ruth my mother,
the adventure of living is boundless. Thank you.

Acknowledgments

A word of gratitude.

Pat Lynch, Joanna Francis, and Mark Levy helped shape this book and bring it to completion. Each one of you made an invaluable contribution. Thank you.

Through our work together, my clients who trusted me and gave me opportunity, taught me about creating new organizational futures. You have been the best learning theater in the world. Thank you.

My global community of friends are the always renewing network of discovery, meaning, development and purpose. You uplift me and make this earthly journey evermore precious. Thank you.

CONTENTS:

- How Ideas Inspire Movements
- Every Day Brings Its Choice Points: You Don't Have to Be a Gladiator
- Exponential learning
- The Creative Bungee-Jump and the Seven-rung Ladder

Where we discover what mental models are and why creating a new future requires building new mental models.

- Can You Turn up the Lights?
- Mental Models and the Games of Life
- My Meryl Moment in Toronto: Which 90% Loss Do You Prefer?
- Are You the Commercial Airline Captain or the Day Trader on Wall Street?

Where we apply the Air Force debrief ritual to build a practice that can save your business and your life.

- Jeff Bezos, Bill Gates, the Air Force and the Law of the Tree
- Getting from the Bottom to the Top of the Class
- Building the Forensic Debrief Practice to Enter the Learning Zone
- Escape the Monty Syndrome: Are You Productive or Just Busy?
- Level Four Listening on the Path to a Billion Dollars

Portal 6: The Art and Science of Creating Breakthroughs   95

Where we explore the power of your Control Field and the virtuous cycle that creates breakthroughs.

• Your Control and Influence Fields
• The Metaphysics of a Strategy Workshop
• Creating Breakthroughs by Escaping Conventional Thinking
• Value-defined Work and the New Paradigm

Portal 7: Begin With the Future   109

Where we develop the outcomes mindset and discover the power of three horizons thinking.

• Inputs, Outcomes, and Reclaiming a Life
• From Frankfurt to Palo Alto, the Three Horizons
• Strategy, Back from the Future
• Process Choreography and the Alchemy of a Strategy Workshop

---

Portal 8: The Opportunity Zone   123

Where we focus on the power of Big Bang learning and discover windows of opportunity.

• My Big Bang Learning Moment
• Your Window of Opportunity (WOO)
• Your Once in a Lifetime Opportunity
• What Is the Most Difficult "Thing" in the World?

Portal 9: The Transformation Agent   139

In which we learn about the drivers for change, the process of adult learning and how to transform broken conversations to address unmet needs.

• The Wow Multiplier
• The Triangle of Change
• The Descartes Trap and the Four Stages of Adult Learning and Transformation
• Samoan Circle in Shanghai—Converting Complaints into Proposals
• An In-Flight Diplomacy Seminar on the Way to Boston

Portal 10: The Wings of Purpose   165

In which we define mission, vision, and purpose, and discover the power of culture.

• What Jim the Beachcomber Can Teach All of Us
• The Purpose-inspired Organization
• Do You Know Yourself?
• What Comes Before MVP
• Give Your Strategy Wings
• The Contribution Pivot

Portal 11: Building a Future in the Three-story House of Work   185

Where we explore a new thinking architecture and a template for action and growth.

• The Three Buckets of Value and Are You the One Out of Ten?
• Diagnostic Dexterity: What Problem Are You Trying to

Preface

Since the beginning of time, human beings have been fascinated by the future. We are wired to anticipate what is about to happen and what is possible in the next minute, the next hour, tomorrow, next week, and next year. We imagine "what if?" scenarios, wondering if we can influence and shape events, and we pursue our preferred pictures of what tomorrow will look like. Waking up each day to new possibilities has always been the propelling force of life, creativity and love.

At age 14, I was fully awakened to the power of this inquiry about the future. During the Yom Kippur war in October 1973, Israel faced a surprise attack that threatened its existence. Because most adults in our kibbutz were called to the army to help save the country, my teenage friends and I assumed responsibility for the livelihood of our community. My work in the avocado orchard proved to be an exhilarating experience: in the context of our country's fight for its survival, our work as young adults took on new meaning. Overnight we became responsible for the continuance of our own lives as well as for the future of the kibbutz.

My father was the Secretary General of our kibbutz. Every night he convened a meeting to discuss the situation, share details about what was going on, and engage people in conversations to help us overcome the shock and trauma of the war. He asked questions. He listened. He offered a point of view. He taught me the value of leading by facilitating conversations.

As the war moved to its resolution, the conversations began to center around the terrible loss and grief the country was experiencing and to give rise to stories of extraordinary heroism and determination. People talked about their worries and concerns about what tomorrow would bring and what the future would hold. Hope as well as anxiety filled the air.

I realized then that people have the power to shape events, that everybody wants their desired future, and that we all are agents who together create what tomorrow will look like.

I saw the role of leaders as shaping events. With this insight, I realized that these two words—leadership and future—are inseparable. To lead means to enable tomorrow, to find a path forward, and to create the future.

The inquiry into the future and leadership became central during my high school years. As I led youth movement activities and managed the school magazine, I had two guiding questions: "What do we want to cause?" and "What do we want to create?"

When I enrolled in the Israeli Air Force, the fighter pilot training exposed me to the economics of learning and performance. As a result, my inquiry into leadership and the future expanded to incorporate ideas about how to accelerate learning and achieve top performance.

These ongoing inquiries evolved to guide a lifelong multidisciplinary quest into the realms of the human potential, purpose, spirituality, and personal and organizational growth and effectiveness. My exploration led me to new understandings about strategy, innovation and emergent fields of knowledge. Like a kaleidoscope that reveals a shape briefly as it comes into focus and clarity before transforming into a new configuration, the nature of my multi-faceted pursuit of meaning, purposeful growth and the future has been characterized by change and evolution.

I have had the privilege of teaching in countries all over the world and helping senior executive teams re-gear and reinvigorate some of the most admired companies in business today. The content of this book is framed around two questions: "What creates new futures?" and "How can you and your team or your family co-create the best possible future?"

The goal of this book is to awaken you to the opportunities presented by your own inquiry about the future, and to encourage you to unleash the full potential of your creative power by practicing the art of conversation. Throughout this journey I will share my discoveries, and the strategies and frameworks I have applied to help senior executives and their teams achieve extraordinary breakthroughs that led to game-changing results.

A Note About the Title of the Book

Why *Create New Futures*? What is the distinctive point of *new* futures?

Though some may think the title is an oxymoron, the fact is that too many people and teams simply recycle their old futures, repeating familiar patterns, experiencing the same mistakes, and reliving the same struggles and pains. Such repetitive old futures were depicted in the 1993 movie *Groundhog Day*, in which Bill Murray's character relives the same day again and again. For too many people and teams, this allegory is their reality.

How does one know that one is not living the *Groundhog Day* scenario, but rather progressing and moving forward to create new futures?

You experience new challenges and make new mistakes. You encounter new problems to solve, ask different questions, and build additional skills and capacities. These actions, together with the new outcomes you experience, will tell you that you are living in a new future, not a recycled one.

In this book I will share how I have helped leaders and teams create new futures that are more exhilarating and far-reaching than they had imagined possible.

A Note About the Structure of the Book

This book does not adhere to a linear, chronological story. Thus you can extract immediate value simply by turning to any page and reading for a few minutes. This approach was intentional, and I share my thinking here briefly because it reflects the evolution of my discovery journey. Old movies like *Ben Hur* and *The Ten Commandments* begin a storyline, follow with an intermission, and then continue the chronology of the plot timeline. Somewhere in the mid-1980s and early 1990s, however, script writers began to employ the innovation of retracing up and down the timeline.

The evolution of this medium caught my attention because it is a reflection of the development of the human capacity to become more universal and less locally based, less time-bound and more adaptive and timeline-flexible.

It also demonstrates audiences' growing sophistication. The public at large seems to be amenable to abandon the Newtonian cause and effect linearity and ready to embrace a more complex network appreciation. The "Digital Natives" who were born in the post-Internet age are not bound by alphabetical order. Their brains have been wired into the Internet topography, where every word and idea has become a clickable portal that furthers the search for a deeper exploration. We all are now experiencing this discovery by getting used to reading in the middle and going with the flow of our interests. For this reason, I have built this book around portals, rather than chapters.

We no longer are bound by the linear cause and effect universe. Instead, we have the freedom to entertain mind-bending ideas. The legacy view that the past defines the future has been overlaid by a "flying upside down" view that contemplates a reverse flow in which the future reframes the past. What an exciting philosophical and spiritual concept!

In my workshops, my clients experience this new-found ability when we engage in the Sacred Stories Circle. In this process I ask people to share formative experiences that contain teachable insights. I use them to demonstrate how we can attach new meaning and significance to an earlier experience from the vantage point of our current content and appreciation. This is a simple example of how we can enable the present and future to update our past.

The point of this example of how I help clients expand their thinking is to free you to explore this book any way you choose. Just as the moments and experiences described in this book trace back and forth in time, so, too, I invite you to let your interests guide your discovery journey.

The vignettes that follow are all part of my discovery journey instigated by the propelling inquiry of this book: what creates the future? I have integrated my personal and professional experiences to provide immediacy of access, to offer a practical translation of ideas, and to demonstrate how I have applied these techniques in my work. I hope this approach will inspire you to become more purposefully present in your life than you are now.

More than ever, humanity now needs people who are open and prepared to imagine, create and sustain new futures. This is a time of great transformative change. It demands our best imagination, courage and creativity.

My task is to inspire you to be tomorrow's agent, and to create conversations that birth a new future.

Let's get started.

Portal 1

The Leadership Leverage

Where we discover what true leaders do and how you can begin to create a new future for yourself and your organization.

A Leader's Job

A leader's most important job is to create the future.

Every leader must ask, "Of all the possible futures before us, what kind of future do we most want? And, what must we do to transform ourselves and our marketplace so we can create that future?"

What mechanism enables people to create the future? Specifically, what allows you to achieve the future you desire for your business? How will you create the future you envision with your team?

Similarly, by what means can you excite your family to imagine the future you desire?

Creating the future, especially in business, might appear to be difficult and unnerving. But it can be easier than you think. One device—a miracle device—will take you there.

What is this device? Conversation.

Conversations are game-changers. Through conversations

we transform ourselves, those around us, and our environments. Ultimately, conversations allow us to shape possibilities, choose the best future imaginable and make it a reality.

But if using conversation as a future-building tool is so powerful and easy, why don't we see more executive teams innovating? Why don't we see more people realizing their capabilities and expressing their genius in ways that alter their lives and their environments for the better?

The answer is simple. Too many people and teams engage in mediocre conversations. Actually, it's worse than that. Many people waste time in toxic, debilitating discussions.

They focus on trivia. They mix the strategic with the tactical. Instead of listening deeply, they engage in circular, repetitive arguments. They focus on petty matters. They look backwards. They accuse and blame instead of solve and create.

Then there are the conversations that fundamentally are different.

These are conversations that open people's minds, help them look forward, and impel them to create meaning and see possibilities. They are about building what's important for everyone involved. These conversations create miracles: spontaneous change, rapid transformation, and profound results.

A conversation can transform the seemingly impossible so it becomes doable. It can make the difficult easy. It can awaken and prompt us, in an instant, to reach agreement by seeing a solution that previously we had been unable to imagine.

Conversations are the human-made miracles that move the world forward every day in small and big ways.

This book will help you initiate and direct conversations that bring out people's most innovative nature. It includes conversations that I have facilitated in my strategic innovation consulting work with some of the biggest organizations in the world, such as Alcoa, Chevron, Cisco, DuPont, General Mills, Hewlett-Packard, Lufthansa, and Procter & Gamble. You will discover how to apply the powerful conversation frameworks that I use with my clients to create a future-focused growth mindset.

You can add powerful conversation frameworks such as these to your conversation toolkit: the emergent conversation, the choreographed conversation, the divergent conversation, the convergent conversation, the foreground and the background conversations, the WHAT, WHY, and HOW conversations.

In my consulting work, for example, I follow the path of least resistance and use emergent or unstructured conversations to uncover where the "energy potential" to mobilize change is greatest.

In contrast, to accelerate diagnostic discovery and apply its insights into prescriptive formulation, I choreograph a series of specific problem-solving conversational steps.

Some of these conversation frameworks can be applied one-on-one, while others are designed to work with teams, or even entire organizations.

Whatever framework you select, because we lead others by leading ourselves, the first conversation is the one we have internally. This book invites you to discover yours. The following portals are written to inspire you to help people and organizations create compelling new futures by adopting and developing the leadership device of conversation.

Insight:

- Conversation is a future-building tool.
- Conversations create miracles by facilitating spontaneous change and rapid transformation.

Developing a conversation about the future has become increasingly essential. Executives, entrepreneurs, employees and organizations of all sizes and types are experiencing remarkable transitions. Change is no longer constant; it is accelerating. Without strong leadership, an organization can teeter between success and failure. The margins of separation between defeat and triumph, chaos and clarity, breakdowns and breakthroughs are exceedingly thin and quick to change.

Within this shape-shifting environment arise extraordinary opportunities that must be seized quickly, or they will vanish.

How do you organize yourself, your team or your company to recognize and respond to these ephemeral opportunities? How do you leverage them to create your desired future?

Through conversation.

It is said that you don't build a business; you build the people and the people build the business.

But how do you build people? Through conversation.

What Is Superior to Unleashing Your Inner Einstein?

Anne is a divisional director of a fast growing company. Known for her ability to combine both the human and the numbers sides of the business, she had progressed quickly through the ranks. During my first meeting with her I asked, "Where is the point of leverage for you as a leader?"

She thought for a few seconds before replying, "My leadership leverage is in how I allocate my resources."

I use challenge questions like, "Where is the point of leverage for you as a leader?" to create a space for executives to revitalize their work by thinking in new ways. There are two reasons why such questions are so effective in re-energizing leaders to think anew.

First, executives are extremely busy. To get their attention immediately, I introduce a new framework by asking a question they have not considered before. This approach forces them to stop and think. As a result, we are able to enter into a different, more expansive space where they can find new ways to energize their leadership.

Second, executives tend to respond positively to questions that appeal to their competitive nature and sense of pride. Posing a challenge question causes them to think, "So what if I've never considered this approach? I am quite capable of thinking on my feet and answering in-the-moment questions I haven't pondered before."

The reaction to a challenge question is instantaneous. It breaks predictability and boredom. Executives who were sitting comfortably on their intellectual armchairs fall off immediately as we engage in a new and freshly stimulated conversation.

To create a new future, true leaders shake off old ideas and find fresh ways of thinking. Consider a salt shaker. If you want the salt to come out, you have to shake the container. Similarly, for a new future to emerge, you must agitate your thinking with new ideas.

Einstein said, "We cannot solve our problems with the same thinking we used when we created them." My objective is to awaken the little Einstein inside each leader I meet.

You might be thinking, "I am not an Einstein. I don't have an inner Einstein." I understand that reaction. But you do have YOU inside. Too many people spend their lives hiding, suppressing their best ideas, playing it safe. Creating a new future requires that you shake up and free your thinking. Unleashing *you* is the inner Einstein I am asking you to liberate.

How do you introduce new ideas to shake up your thinking?

Asking a different question is one way to trigger new thinking. When I meet with you, I seek to open a greater vista for you. I ask you to rethink how you look at what you do, your work, and your leadership. I prod, I challenge, and I become as animated as necessary to get us into a new space.

Creating a new future requires different ways of seeing and thinking. A full cup cannot hold another drop. Rather than asking you to empty your existing cup, I prefer to take the faster route by helping you create another, bigger cup that has plenty of room for new contents.

The challenge question I asked Anne about her leadership leverage created a new thinking cup for her, a vast, clear space for fresh thoughts. Once I had her attention and she expanded her thinking, we were able to elevate our conversation. Here's what happened next.

I replied, "Resource allocation as your leadership leverage is a great answer, Anne. Now can you imagine an even higher point of leverage?"

A fascinating dialogue ensued. Anne knew that I was challenging her thinking. She loves to play the game and is not defensive. She values the insight gained by taking full advantage of the learning opportunity at hand more highly than being right in the first attempt. This characteristic has contributed both to her success and to her team's appreciation of her leadership style.

"I get to define our mission and objectives," she said thoughtfully, "That's a higher leverage point, because they inform my resource allocation."

Anne looked at me with a victorious smile. I know this smile. It's the one that says, "I don't need you to tell me that I nailed it."

By following this conversation, we can see how Anne developed her thinking framework. Her second response shows she recognized the hierarchy of questions: mission answers the "why" question, objectives address the "what," and resource allocation specifies the "how."

She looked at me with smiling eyes, confident she had delivered a checkmate.

"Yes," I agreed, "you discovered the right answer. Now I am looking for a different framing, Anne. I am asking you to push your thinking envelope still further. What's another way to articulate what you have just said?"

My response is an example of the affirmative challenge technique that I use to provoke new thinking. Specifically, the first word I use in my reply is the most important word in any conversation: YES. Without a "yes" first, there is no continuing conversation and there can be no new future.

Anne looked at me puzzled, as though the bird she had just caught had escaped from her hand.

"What's another way to state what I have just said? Do you mean what's another way to say that my leadership leverage is defining our mission and objectives?" she paraphrased.

Paraphrasing is another form of "yes," and is an important element in the call and response of a conversation. It also is an indicator of active listening.

"Yes, Anne, by defining your mission and objectives, you define... what?" That is the hint I gave to encourage and nudge her into the new thinking space she had created.

As Anne grappled with the riddle, I purposely maintained the state of suspended silence. This point was a pivotal moment in our conversation: millions of neurons in Anne's brain were firing to establish the connection that would allow her to solve the riddle. These millions of neurons and the calories they were consuming were etching this moment into her memory. Such moments are critical for leaders to inspire others to create forward movement.

"You are annoying me, Aviv! Give me another hint," Anne said.

"If mission statement and objectives are more than just a slide that you print, post on the corporate wall and pray will make a difference, then they are part of... what?" I asked.

"Well, they are part of our daily conversation. They are a frame of reference for our discussions."

"That's your answer, Anne. Your leadership leverage is that you get to frame the conversation. You therefore must ask yourself and your team questions such as, 'What is the conversation we are in? Is this the right conversation or should we be engaging in a different one? And if indeed this is the right conversation, are we framing the discussion in the best possible way to help us create the desired outcomes?'"

I continued, "As a leader, you get to shape the conversation agenda and its character. This is a critical leadership insight. Imagine the competitive differentiation between one leader who fully appreciates that leadership is the power to shape the conversation, and another who believes that by allocating resources she has declared her priorities. It's an unequal fight. To use an Air Force analogy, it's like an F16 fighting an A4 Skyhawk. I have flown the Skyhawk, and I can tell you it's no fight at all. The F16's maneuverability envelope is far superior to that of the Skyhawk."

As Anne discovered through our dialogue, true leaders

create and shape conversations. Doing so is their highest point of leverage, and is the tool that enables them to achieve their goals most effectively.

Insights:

- New questions enable you to enter a vastly expanded thinking space.
- To see a new future, you must agitate your thinking with fresh ideas.
- To lead is to frame the conversation. As a leader, your job is to shape the conversation agenda.

Practice application:

Recognize that as a leader your greatest leverage is creating and shaping the conversation. Too many teams are ineffective because they engage in circular conversations that lead nowhere.

Get into the habit of asking yourself and your team these questions and using these approaches:
- What is the conversation we are in?
- Is this the conversation we should be in at this time, or is there a different, more critical one in which we must engage?
- Ask "why" questions to clarify cause and to elicit meaning and mission.
- Formulate "what" explorations to frame objectives.
- Propose "how" inquiries to determine tactics and resource allocation.

The Currency of Work: Are You Prepared to Suspend Disbelief?

I am meeting the leadership team responsible for the supply chain and procurement function of one of the largest oil and gas companies in the world to help them update their organizational strategy and priorities. They know their business well, and they are very good at what they do.

"What do you do at work?" I ask the leadership team.

Looking around the room, I see 24 people staring at me. In their eyes is a look of puzzled surprise that says, "What do you mean, what do we do at work? We do our jobs!"

I am used to seeing this look in response to a question that sounds pedestrian. So I ask again, "Please, tell me what you do at work."

Asking a simple question requires courage and conviction. I must demonstrate that I mean what I say and say what I mean.

Many managers have a mild to severe condition called "the theater agent syndrome." It's the "I've seen everything there is to see, so there is nothing new you can show me" mindset. It is a defensive reaction to continuous change that can create a dangerous state of mind because it blinds you, shutting you off from possibilities. Managers who feel that they have seen it all tend to become cynical, assuming there is nothing new that will impress or move them.

How do I introduce new insights to help free managers from this dysfunctional way of thinking?

First, I must have the courage of my convictions. Cynicism is a lie. Deep inside, most people want to make a difference. They want to contribute and to participate in meaningful work. In my work I give the teams I help an incentive to believe in what they do. I ask them to suspend disbelief; I summon them to be in the presence of their revitalized and renewed selves. By expressing my belief that they matter and that their presence is purposeful and significant, I give them permission to look deeply into themselves, beyond the cynicism that holds them back.

Second, to bring a new consideration and a fresh point of view, I ask the most fundamental of questions: "What do you do at work?"

"We develop our strategy and we hold our teams accountable to execute it," says one executive.

"Yes, and what else?"

This is a phrase I use to encourage people to explore openly and daringly. "Yes" is positive and affirming, while "What else?" pushes them to expand their frame of thinking rather than settle for their first thought. "Yes, and what else?" is an effective prod to encourage divergent exploration.

"We learn about the needs of our business partners and develop solutions to address their priorities. Ultimately, we help the business win," another manager says.

"Yes. Great point. And what else do you do at work?"

"Well, we fulfill the demands of our customers," is the third reply.

"Absolutely, that's a critical aspect of your work. What else do you do?"

At this point people begin to warm up and fire more answers in my direction.

"We develop our people."

"We respond to crises and fix problems."

"We take customer feedback and review our results."

"Great answers," I respond. "Let's see if I captured what you said you do at work. You develop a strategy. You deploy and execute the strategy. You hold your teams accountable. You fulfill customer demands. You address concerns and priorities of internal partners. You develop your people and you solve problems. Now, as you reflect on all these activities, what is the unifying principle? What is a comprehensive way to describe all that you do at work?"

There's a moment of silence. Then a senior executive speaks. "The unifying element of all these things is communication. Every aspect of our work involves communicating internally in our organization and externally with other groups. Everything we do at work begins and ends with communication."

"Yes, exactly! How can we capture this insight in a word that's bigger than communication?" I allow a moment of suspended silence. You can almost hear the neural fireworks in people's heads as they compete to resolve the riddle.

I frame the answer. "Communication is a one-dimensional word. I am looking for another word, a bigger word than communication. That word is conversation.

"What you do as leaders and managers is create and connect conversations that mobilize organizational action. Conversation is the currency of work. Creating and leading purposeful conversations is how you produce results at work."

Resolving the mystery brings relief, and the tension that had built up in the last few minutes relaxes. Immediately I take the next step, knowing that we must not waste the moment of relief. I use the energy of the moment to deepen the realization by following up with a series of questions:

"Why is conversation important? What is different when we realize that creating and connecting conversations is the essence of work? How does this insight help our work?"

After pausing for a few seconds to let the group internalize the questions, I ask further, "Simply put, how are we better off by reminding each other that we come to work to create conversations?"

An open exploration unfolds, and a series of responses are offered. With every reply, these leaders internalize more deeply the ideas that creating conversations is what they do at work and that conversation is the currency of work. I love facilitating discoveries like this one, where executives create their own insights and revelations. They tend to retain what they discover and articulate themselves far longer than they remember what I tell them.

I then bring the conversation into convergence by summarizing three critical points:

"First, by recognizing that what we do at work is create conversations, we draw attention to the anatomy of conversation. It represents two-way traffic that creates a complete loop. We pay attention to the inquiry and the response; we address the concern; and we reply to the request. We make sure to close the conversation loop by addressing clients' and partners' needs and opportunities.

"Second, by embracing conversation as the currency of work, we look at the world and the way we work through a new lens. We ask, 'How clear and effective are the conversations we create? What results do our conversations produce?' Effective conversations increase the velocity of movement from inquiry to resolution; they deliver results that satisfy the initial intent.

"Third, by realizing that the meaning of work is to create and shape conversations, we quickly recognize that a new future for the organization must begin with creating different conversations. If all we do is repeat the same old conversation, by definition we remain stuck in our present situation, unable to move forward to our desired new future.

"To discover and unlock new possibilities, we first must ask a new question and present a fresh canvas that enables a different conversation. The future emerges through our dialogue."

The leadership team is now on point with me. We have entered into a new conversation. The workshop begins.

"Let's be present in our conversations. And let's begin by exploring what critical conversations we must include in this strategy effort."

Insights:

- Cynicism is a lie. Deep inside, most people want to make a difference.
- The essence of work is creating and connecting conversations that address needs and produce movement and results.
- Creating a new future requires that we engender a different conversation. No new conversation means no new future.

Inviting you to be mindfully present and to explore the new conversations you want to create is the purpose of this book. I am asking you to bring a heightened level of awareness to the conversations you enable at work and in your life.

I propose that you take responsibility for the conversations you fashion. They are your contributions, the means by which you create meaning and value.

The contributions you bring to the world every day result from the conversations you create. They must begin with the one you have with yourself, the way you think and the story you tell yourself.

Practice application:

- Suspend disbelief and ask your team to do likewise. Believing that all of you matter and are here for a purpose is how you begin to make a difference.
- Use the "Yes, and what else?" question to invite people to explore openly and daringly.
- Use puzzle questions and riddles to engage stake-holders. People tend to retain what they discover and articulate themselves much longer than they remember what you tell them.
- Make sure you close the conversation loop: validate that you've heard the need; address the concern; and/or reply to the request.
- Evaluate the effectiveness of your conversations. What results do they produce?

Your Portal Into the Future

Do others find your conversations interesting or boring? Do these interactions make you feel energized or tired? Are you renewed through your exchanges, or do they leave you feeling worn out?

Let me be more specific. In your personal and professional

life, you become known for the quality, the character and the charisma of your conversation. Do your conversations create impact, or are they devoid of meaning? Do your conversations open the door to future possibilities or slam it shut before they can be recognized?

Do I have your attention? Are you ready to embark on the work of creating your new futures through high impact, meaningful conversations?

Conversation:

- is where hope finds realization.

- is the oasis of meaning.

- enables you to match solutions with the needs they are meant to serve.

- uncovers what is going on inside of you and what is yours to do.

- builds the bridge from possibility to realization.

- creates meaning, which according to Dr. Viktor Frankl is the most powerful catalyst in the world.

- converts confusion into clarity, turns setbacks into actionable learning, and transforms objections into supportive collaboration.

- is where ideas are born and carried out to actualization.

- fosters understanding, mutual respect and trust.

- becomes the crucible for insights that generate forward movement.

- is a portal into the future.

Portal 2

What Is the Work That Creates New Futures?

Where we find a connection between the wisdom of Mandela and a NASA astronaut that enables us to better appreciate the transformative work required to shape the future.

I t is 1993, on a hot July afternoon, when I arrive at JFK with my wife, our six-year-old son, and seven suitcases. Between my wife and I we carry $12,000. Nothing else is secured or certain: not a job, not a salary. Any rational analysis of our situation would reveal immediately that it is craziness of the highest degree. Sure, we can rent a house and buy food for a few months. All I have is an improbable dream to create a new life for my family, to win our freedom.

My hopes are to learn from a great teacher, and to use my skills and gifts to make it in America. There is no ticket back. There is no plan B. There is no support system. I must find a way quickly to create this new life out of very little. But before I can persuade my wife that things will work out, that we are going to be okay, that we will succeed, I must find a cab to take us from JFK to LaGuardia to catch our connection to Palm Beach. I am standing on the road waving frantically, but no taxi driver who sees all our luggage will pick us up.

I finally persuade a good-hearted taxi driver of Indian descent: "We'll push three suitcases onto the back seat and lie on them and

I'll pay you double." God bless his heart; we are on our way. Our American odyssey begins.

What New Future Do You Hope to Create?

Leaders of organizations large and small ought to reflect on this question about the future. In our roles as parents, teachers, mentors and people who strive to shape our own personal futures, we too must ask and answer this question.

What do I mean by a "new future?" What is the work that creates new futures?

We work to create a future that:

- improves conditions for the people involved.
- solves an intractable problem.
- develops new possibilities.
- builds creative products, services, and solutions.
- expands business and opens new markets.
- resolves conflicts and fosters agreements and understanding.
- reconciles and enables peace.
- generates prosperity and expands freedom.
- heals and enables wellbeing and joy.
- fosters talent and builds leadership.
- enables sustained fulfillment and happiness.

This list describes a future desired by those who want to improve life for themselves and the people they love. We all grapple with problems and challenges, and we hope to find new possibilities and fulfilling experiences that produce personal success and joy.

In business we work to create new products, solutions and services, to open up new markets, to expand opportunities and to build wealth and wellbeing.

How do we shape and create such a future?

Through conversation.

By connecting unrelated conversations and by creating new conversations, we free people's imaginations and unleash their talents to realize their desired future. Through conversation we solve problems, develop new ideas and options, and foster leadership that liberates creativity, freedom and growth.

My mission is to encourage you to take on the leadership work of creating new futures by bringing novel conversations to life.

An Invisible Witness to the Presidential Palace: How Mandela Shaped the Future

When Nelson Mandela walked into the presidential palace for his first meeting with South African President F.W. de Klerk, he had been a prisoner for 26 years.

What Mandela understood perhaps better than anyone else was that leadership is determined not by a title, but by one's capacity to shape the conversation.

As de Klerk and Mandela sat down in that destiny-shaping moment, leadership was available to both. Engaging in conversation with de Klerk, Mandela worked to shape a peaceful future for his country by explaining the conditions that would enable all South Africans—blacks and whites—to live together.

President F.W. de Klerk listened in a way that his predecessors had not. As a result, the two men were able to open the door to new possibilities for their country and their people.

Leadership is not defined by a role or title. At that meeting, we saw leadership demonstrated by both men. With his capacity, clarity of vision, and moral courage to shape the conversation, Mandela embodied leadership. And de Klerk had the capacity to listen, understand and allow leadership to manifest.

You probably have seen the optical illusion image of two profiles that also look like a vase. When you blink you see two profiles; when you blink again your brain reverses the figure and the space in between so you can see the vase. Shifting the focus allows you to alternate between the faces and the vase. Let's take this alternating focus into the meeting between Mandela and de Klerk.

Imagine you are in the presidential palace as an invisible witness to the dialogue between these two men. In the foreground, you observe their faces and expressions. Now you blink to shift the focus. As both figures recede into the background, the conversation itself moves into the foreground. The dance of the spoken words and their meaning, the intonation and the cadence, and the interaction in the middle become the focus.

Can you see how, in that moment, the conversation is the leader that opens a new future?

Traditionally we associate leadership with a person, such as a man or woman carrying the title of CEO, General, President whose role is accompanied by authority, power and influence. However, shifting your focus and perception as described above reveals that the conversation itself is the leader of new possibilities and their actualization.

What do I mean by saying *conversation is the leader of possibilities*?

The conversation between Mandela and de Klerk allowed them to take each other's measure and to begin building trust and confidence. It led them to believe that they could work together. And it revealed how dialogue can bring about reconciliation. The future of South Africa was shaped by this conversation and those that followed. The possibility of peace eventually became a reality.

Think about important conversations in your life, those that offered new insights, shaped your worldview and beliefs, and perhaps led you to directional choices. Now imagine just one such life-centering conversation that specifically influenced your direction in life. Perhaps it was a conversation with a manager, a teacher, a coach or a parent that resulted in a desired possibility becoming a reality. As you recall the conversation, allow the blinking of your eyes technique to shift the figures and background. Can you see that in that special moment of high impact in your life, the emergent dynamic of the interaction, namely the conversation, was the leadership alchemy that transformed possibility into reality?

In our strategy and innovation workshops with clients, I apply the power of this insight that the conversation is the invisible leader. Invariably, I observe that the conversation itself leads and creates possibilities previously not imagined by its participants. The emergent conversations during our workshops create connections and permutations that give birth to a new future for teams and their organizations.

On its own, an organization has no inherent meaning. Rather, its significance and power are created through conversation. In fact, an organization is the sum total of the conversations among its people. In the following pages I will share a series of pivotal conversations that have led executive teams to identify and leverage breakthrough opportunities.

I invite you to discover how to shape the future by purposefully choreographing your own conversations.

Insights:

- Conversation is the leader of possibilities.
- The conversation you create begins with your internal dialogue, in the way you think and the story you tell yourself.
- The capacity to shape the conversation engenders leadership; a title does not.
- By virtue of its ability to open a new future, a conversation can lead.

A Leadership Conversation at 36,000 Feet

Next time you are traveling by airplane, recognize that the person seated next to you is carrying a treasure, a lesson for you. How will you obtain this treasured lesson? Through conversation.

I board the flight home from a strategy summit with a Hewlett-Packard leadership team in Houston. As we taxi from the gate, I discover the man seated next to me, Nicholas, is not just a NASA senior engineer, but an astronaut. In fact, he has been to space more than once.

On his laptop, Nicholas shows me a photo of the Earth that he had taken with his own camera as his shuttle orbited the planet.

Now, I have seen countless photographs of the Earth on TV and in magazines. Countless photographs. Thousands of them. But to see a photo of the Earth taken from space by the man sitting next to me offers the opportunity of a whole new perspective and restores the magic to the image. I experience it with fresh eyes. As Nicholas describes how thin the atmosphere is and how fragile the ecosystem, I am listening intently and deeply. I take in his own profound experience of seeing this actuality from space.

"What are you working on now?" I ask.

"Today I consulted with the engineers working on Orion, which is the space program NASA designed to replace the retired shuttle fleet. Orion will carry astronauts farther into the solar system than ever before and return them safely to Earth. I do my consulting in a dual capacity. I consult as an astronaut and as a human factor engineer."

"Human factor engineer?"

"Human factor engineering is about designing devices and systems for human use. I specialize in the interface between humans and robotics."

I realize I am sitting next to an incredible treasure. Nicholas carries a universe of experience and knowledge I am not likely to encounter ever again for an uninterrupted four hours. The thrill of finding this jewel drives my next inquiry. I want to understand the principles that govern the interface between humans and robots. I want to understand how the two interact and converse.

Why is pursuing this line of inquiry so important to me?

I'm enthralled by the ways people master their domain of knowledge. Uncovering how they do it is a rapid way to unlock the treasure hidden inside a lifetime of experience.

"What principles govern effective human interface with robotics?" I ask.

Nicholas takes a moment. He has never been asked this question before, and works to formulate an understandable answer to someone who knows nothing about his field. I am getting close to the treasure.

"There are four principles we must follow to design effective human interface with robotics: consistency, compatibility, simplicity, and new mental models.

"Consistency is critical because the logic you apply in designing a system must be followed dependably, right through from beginning to end, so as not to confuse the user.

"Compatibility is the essence of user-friendly design. The application and usage of tools and functionalities should be easily and comfortably accessible in real time in every situation and for every need.

"Simplicity is vital for dealing with complex systems. You must not complicate the complex. There is a difference between 'complex' and 'complicated.' A simplified process helps you manage a complex structure.

"Finally, a system must enable new mental models to open possibilities and give permission for greater versatility, scope and functionality."

Nicholas shared his treasure with me by effectively compressing 20 years of learning into an easily understandable conversation. I can't wait to discover its meaning! A couple of hours after returning home, I realize the gift Nicholas had shared.

The core principles of all domains of knowledge are connected. For example, by understanding climate systems you can gain new insights into the dynamics of organizational life. By understanding a human cell, you get clues as to the workings of the greater universe.

The four principles Nicholas framed as key to enabling effective human interactions with robots are just as essential for the leadership conversation.

1. **Consistency.** As a leader, you must be consistent. Consistency makes you reliable in the eyes of your people and helps them understand your message, see you as being trustworthy and be willing to support and work with you toward your vision.

2. **Compatibility.** You are expected to frame a strategy compatible with changing needs and environments. Your communication must be well-suited and relevant to all stakeholders. To create alliances and foster collaboration with diverse people, you must be an adaptive leader, ready to adjust your style and method of engagement to meet their needs.

3. **Simplicity.** Your leadership conversation must be simple, focusing on what matters most. People look to you for help in sense-making that leads to action. To be an impactful leader you must offer a simple bridge from clear vision to effective action.

4. **New mental models.** Finally, you create a platform for effective leadership by being consistent, compatible and conveying a simple message. With this platform you can help your people be open to new possibilities by reframing any situation. Leaders who are proficient at reframing enable and give birth to new mental models. They provide the portals that allow us to change ourselves and refashion the world.

Treasure Hunts and the Spider-Man Story

How prepared are you to hunt for treasures like the one Nicholas shared with me?

All around you are people whose experiences generate treasures of wisdom. You may be unaware of those gems until an extraordinary event reveals them or a meaningful conversation exposes them.

Chance conversations like the one I had with Nicholas can

be memorable. They make you appreciate the wisdom and brilliance of people you meet. Such spontaneous, emergent dialogues can open doors to powerful insights that engender growth and new possibilities. I have experienced many such memorable conversations that changed me. These dispensers of wisdom include a nuclear submarine engineer, a prominent biotechnologist, a top diplomat, a dog trainer, and a Jesuit priest.

How do these conversations transpire?

I am prepared for, and I actively seek, the treasure nearby. I know that there is a jewel hidden inside the experience of the stranger sitting next to me. My active inquiry often allows me to unearth it.

If I can make the space, if I can create the conversation and ask the pivotal question that helps bring forward the hidden treasure inside the other person, and if I listen intently to discover and capture the meaning-making significance, I am likely to be transformed by a great insight, by beauty, and by new horizons of potential applications.

A week after my conversation with Nicholas I am leading a workshop with 60 Hewlett-Packard managers in Boston. The workshop brief includes a module on the practices of adaptive leadership, a body of work I had developed several years earlier. Today, however, I begin anew. At first I share my conversation with the NASA astronaut at 36,000 feet. In the workshop, the four principles come alive and evolve. That is the nature of emergent conversations. They carry and transfer knowledge, open new horizons of meaning, and guide behavior and action.

Bringing forward the best in people is part of my work to help others create new futures. In the following portals, I share a series of conversations I use to garner the best strengths and wisdom from people sitting around the table.

One such conversation is a special process choreography I call the Sacred Stories Circle. My earlier work with leadership and top talent teams utilized the Sacred Stories Circle as a breakthrough device. Participants share stories of formative moments in their lives to help them discover and decipher their core values, attributes and passions.

In addition to bringing forward the best in people, the Sacred Stories Circle captures teachable morals that have shaped who they are and how they see the world. These stories provide fortifying and revealing insights, and I use this process to demonstrate how we can use stories to mine for learning insights. Even when people have been working together for a long time, they are amazed to discover how much they do not know about each other. The process reveals some of the profound events and challenging setbacks their team members overcame successfully throughout their personal and professional journeys.

During WebEx's rapid growth years and before it was acquired by Cisco, I led a leadership event for the company's executives that included the Sacred Stories Circle ritual.

For this occasion, I ask the team members to share their Spider-Man stories. I set it up by saying, "You and I would not be where we are without our Spider-Man or Spider-Woman. We all needed help. We all needed someone to stretch out an arm toward us. To give us opportunity. To show us it can be done. To say, 'You can do it.' To believe in us. To raise us up.

"There is a 'Spider-Man' impulse in all of us. We love to help. To make a difference. The receiving is in the giving. When you help someone else, you are being helped as well. Today, I would like us all to share a Spider-Man story, a story about a moment or situation in which someone has helped or even rescued you. I want us to listen to these stories to evoke the extraordinary power we humans have to help each other."

One after another the managers share their Spider-Man stories. Simple stories. Moving stories. Amazing stories.

Perennial messages shine through these story circles:
1. None of us got to where we are on our own.
2. We all have been inspired by someone who gave us a chance.
3. We become great achievers through the help and support of others.
4. Everything special, every unique accomplishment, has been the work of more than one person.

5. One moment, one word, or one sentence has the power to change the course of a person's life.

Here is Stu's Spider-Man story:

"In my elementary school there was this geeky kid who wasn't very capable physically. The problem was that he had a gimp right arm and hand that were considerably weaker, smaller and less dexterous than his left. In gym class, the instructor would often make him sit out of activities because he just couldn't do them, or would sometimes even hurt himself. One time, we were doing flips over the pommel horse. This kid left the springboard, and as his hands hit the pommel, his right arm gave way and he crashed headlong into it. The parallel and high-bars were totally out of his league. Needless to say, he was the brunt of a lot of jokes and an easy mark for the bullies, which in any small town are always in abundance.

"The kid joined an intramural floor-hockey team that played in the lunch league. The teams were picked randomly, and he ended up on a team with one of the school's top jocks, a natural athlete who excelled at every sport he played. The jock basically could score goals on command and was revered for his talent by students and teachers alike.

"During one of these intramural games, the geek kid was running down the right-wing boards and found himself behind the defenders with the jock stick-handling the puck down the left-wing boards. The jock was lining up for a shot, and there was absolutely no doubt he could beat the goalie and score. But instead of firing the puck into the net, the jock passed it to the geeky kid. With no defenders around the goalie, and the goalie focused on the jock, in almost complete disbelief, the geeky kid one-timed the puck hard into the back of the net! SCORE!

"That geeky kid was me. To this day I still can see that orange plastic puck coming across the gym floor in slow motion. I still hear the team and spectators cheering the goal. I still feel the rush and exhilaration of seeing the puck fire into the net while the goalie belatedly moved toward my side of the net. I still feel my heart pumping with joy as the team swarmed me with congratulatory slaps on my back.

"That season I became the highest goal scorer on our team, while the jock had the highest number of assists. Later I became the quarterback and captain of the football team. Although I still had my gimp arm and hand, I was a changed person because of the confidence I had gained in that one split-second when my Spider-Man chose to pass the puck to me instead of shooting it himself.

"He was a true Spider-Man, though to this day, I can't remember his name. My Spider-Man, the man without an identity, impacted my life in ways that I know he is unaware of. However, I will be eternally grateful to him."

Today Stu flies light planes and is one of the brightest and most articulate executives I know. He traces his confidence to this moment when his teammate provided an opportunity for him to succeed.

Insights:

• Spontaneous conversations can open doors to powerful insights that engender growth and new possibilities.

• The core principles of all domains of knowledge are connected. Evolutionary biology carries insights and applications into the field of innovation. Music, math and poetry offer cross-fertilizing revelations. Gardening carries lessons for personal development and growth.

• The experience and wisdom treasures we accumulate become the building blocks of the new future we are capable of building.

Practice application:

• To unlock the treasure hidden inside a lifetime of experience, inquire about the other person's domain of knowledge.

• Ask a pivotal question that helps bring forward the wisdom and knowledge treasure hidden inside the other person.

• Listen intently to discover and capture the meaning-making significance and to decipher how these insights are applicable to your field of inquiry.

• You are here to help others. To help them help themselves. To help them discover that they are here to help the people around them. Ask your team to share their Spider-Man and Spider-Woman stories. Watch them become inspired by each other's stories.

Portal 3

The "What's Next" Ladder

Where we learn that creating a new future requires leaders to generate intellectual firepower.

In a few months I will be celebrating my eighth birthday. Today though, a cold, dreary morning, I am on a bus with my dad on our way to see the heart specialist. After sitting for two hours in the waiting room, we finally see the doctor. I am told to take off my shirt and stand behind the cold machine. The doctor sticks the icy electrocardiogram sensors on my chest. Am I shivering because I am cold or because I am scared? After more waiting we are called back into the room. The doctor never makes eye contact with me as he talks to my father. "Your son's condition is not severe but he needs to be monitored. He is likely to get tired and he should not over-exert himself." My father nods his head as I listen in disbelief. The dark clouds are moving in on me: I've just been given a suspended death sentence. All I care about is playing soccer, running and swimming. Now I am told I can no longer enjoy these activities, which may be dangerous for me.

As we board the bus for the trip home, I remain frozen in shock and fear. My horizon is shrinking rapidly. Though I am bewildered, I am not alone in my confusion. My father has a sure presence about him. A holocaust survivor, he has defied death. He is a resilient and pragmatic man, the eternal optimist. But at this moment he is quiet, and I disappear inside myself, beginning a new internal conversation.

Looking through the bus window on the way home, I watch the rain on the beautiful orchards and fields. Does it rain only outside, or also inside me? I am staring at the rain when I experience an unfamiliar sensation welling up inside. This feeling surprises me at first, though later in life I will come to recognize and welcome it. Surging in my chest is a burning intensity that transforms the implosion inside into a fiery rebelliousness. Although at the time I do not know these words, a spirit of defiance has been awakened. I turn to my father and vow, "You know this will not be. I will run, I will run free..."

And so begins a new conversation.

How Ideas Inspire Movements

In sharing these conversational experiences with you, my guiding premise is that conversations have the power to reveal, to teach, and to lead. I know for a fact that your conversations can uncover ideas and possibilities that lie dormant within you.

To discover the latent knowledge that lies within, you must learn to pay attention when you speak. You may find yourself saying something you have not heard before!

This seemingly radical concept has a biological explanation. As you engage in new conversations, your brain makes new and novel synaptic connections. These new-born circuitries bring forward fresh ideas, suggest viable solutions to previously intractable problems, inspire poetry and creative expression, and unleash innovation breakthroughs.

That is exactly what happens when you are inspired by a new idea. The thrill and the energy release you experience are part of the biological reaction that occurs. New synaptic connections free up your latent energy potential.

What happens when the bio-energetic potential is liberated? What doors do your new synaptic circuitries open for you?

As you get excited and energized, you move into action. Physics teaches us that energy potential is converted into kinetic energy. Thus your ideas inspire movement. This transformation demonstrates the power and potency of conversation.

Here is my radical point: the conversation you start with your team today may unleash the movement that will change your future and possibly create dramatic new experiences for your organization and your customers. As the next portals of the book show, conversation-generated connections, understandings and appreciations can create new futures for you and for your teams.

Insights:

- Conversations have the power to reveal and to teach.
- New synaptic connections in your brain are created when you change the conversation. These new circuitries release energy that can inspire break-through ideas and possibilities.

Every Day Brings Its Choice Points: You Don't Have to Be a Gladiator

Margaret Mead* captured the idea that a conversation can unleash the energy potential that triggers movement when she stated, "Never doubt that a small group of thoughtful, committed citizens can change the world; indeed, it's the only thing that ever has."

With all due respect, I propose to amend Mead's statement to make this radical point: "Never doubt that a *conversation among* a small group of thoughtful, committed citizens can change the world; indeed, it's the only thing that ever has."

---

* *Margaret Mead (1901-1978) popularized the insights of anthropology in modern culture.*

Unfortunately, much of what passes for conversation these days is far from lofty or inspiring. Indeed, the kind of open-ended exploration and discovery inquiry that I engaged in with Nicholas is rare. I choose to create inspiring conversations, and you can, too.

Many of the words people exchange regurgitate what someone repeats about what a third person said about what a fourth person did. This kind of talk cannot possibly create new, inspiring futures. Political talk shows are a case in point. They feature 24/7 arguments designed primarily to increase their ratings by accentuating conflict with the recycled spewing of polarizing positions. Hosts and guests alike tear people up and pull them down in an effort to bring themselves or someone else up. This ploy is as old as time, a modern version of the Roman gladiatorial games where audiences were regaled by one combatant facing a violent confrontation with other gladiators and wild animals.

By my definition, the general political discourse does not qualify as conversation. Why? Because people do not truly listen to themselves or each other. Their words are meant to demean and demolish rather than to encourage learning, foster growth and promote discovery. People engaged in this type of discourse treat words as agents of destruction, like gunfire in the battlefield. They have no interest in weaving threads of inquiry, building new options, or creating meaning and encouraging imaginative tomorrows.

I have little time or patience for degrading discourse. Life is too precious to be squandered in exchanges that demean people. When I humiliate someone, I debase myself. There is no victory in diminishing another person. There is no room for destructive exchanges in my definition of conversation.

Every conversation represents a choice point for us. We must ask, "What is the conversation I am in? Do I choose to continue to participate in it, or do I choose a different conversational path?" You and I have a choice: to engage or disengage. Once we choose to participate in a conversation, we also decide how to engage.

I choose to engage in conversations that discover and reveal, conversations that open possibilities and heal, that elicit the best ideas and strengths in others and lead to innovation breakthroughs. I choose conversations that release us to levels of freedom and creativity well beyond what we had imagined possible.

What conversations do you choose? Will they bring to life the energy potential within you and others?

Insight:

• Every conversation is a choice point. Will you engage or not? If you do, how will you frame the discussion?

Exponential Learning

My fascination with the power of conversation was propelled by my inquiry into learning and how we can enable faster and more long-lasting application and impact.

The traditional approach to learning, which arose during the industrial revolution era in the United States, incorporates a mechanical and industrial bias. Schools became "factories" of learning. The resulting learning and knowledge paradigm says you must learn first before you can speak and before you can do.

The "learn before you speak" paradigm of the traditional educational approach works up to a point in specific situations. However, it is woefully inadequate for purposes of creating new futures. After thinking deeply about the processes of learning and leading, and having applied the insights I gained to my teaching, coaching, and consulting with executive and management teams all around the world for decades, I can attest that the reverse framing is even more powerful.

Instead of following the "learn-so-you-can-do" model, pivot to the "do-so-you-can-learn" approach. "Do-learn" is faster and more potent than "learn-do." The immersive do-learn approach unleashes accelerated brain plasticity, the "synaptic fireworks" that occur with emergent, experiential learning. Indeed, toddlers instinctively apply the "do-learn" approach as they explore their worlds. Unfortunately, that natural discovery process often is stifled once children are placed into a traditional classroom.

While it is true that the "learn-so-you-can-converse" approach serves a necessary and legitimate purpose, the reverse flow of "converse-so-you-can-learn" is a million times faster and more potent, and it delivers a fuller and more holistic development experience.

"Learn-so-you-can-converse" is linear.

"Converse-so-you-can-learn" is exponential.

Why exponential?

Because through conversation you tap into three inexhaustible learning spaces. You learn from the other person; you learn from the dynamic of the conversation; and, perhaps surprisingly, you learn from yourself.

Insights:

- "Do-learn" is faster and more potent than "learn-do."
- "Learn-so-you-can-converse" facilitates linear growth. Exponential learning and growth require a "converse-so-you-can-learn" practices.
- Exponential learning enables you to learn from yourself.

The Conversational Bungee Jump and the Seven-rung Ladder

Here is an example of a conversation that illustrates how you can learn from yourself. The radical point is that you must listen to what you say to find out what is going on inside your process, and to develop the mindset and the conviction that when you pay attention, powerful insights and innovative ideas show up in your conversations.

I apply what I call the "conversational bungee jump" exercise as a technique to help my clients and to build mental prowess and conversational dexterity. The conversational bungee jump helps both them and me develop framing skills that enable us to discover new insights and formulations.

Doug is a gifted coach. We have been engaged in peer coaching for a number of years.

The phone rings and I pick it up, using a direct "hello question" to jump-start our dialogue: "Hey Doug, what are you focusing on today?"

Doug replies right away. "There are two questions every person on Earth asks daily. The first is 'How can I provide for my loved ones?' and the second is, 'What's next?'"

"Yes," I agree. Then I immediately make the mental bungee jump: "There are seven levels to the 'What's next?' question."

"Really? What are they?" Doug replies. I can hear the smile in his voice.

I have been playing with conversational bungee jumps for some 30 years. The exercise is simple. First you state that there are three, four, five, or seven levels of "What's next?" Then you follow through to find out what they are. It is a great way to access your creative unconscious mind, sharpen your mental agility and build intellectual fire power. You create a riddle you are committed to decipher and solve, so you come up with the solution.

I have used this technique to discover and develop some of the most useful frameworks I teach and implement in my consulting practice, including:

- The three-legged stool of breakthrough partnering and collaboration
- The three pillars of trust
- The five buckets of intelligence
- The four chambers of the accountability heart
- The three propulsions of great organizations
- The triangle of change
- The five faces of courage

- The five needs of employees
- The five conflicts
- The five steps to overcoming resistance

I use the conversational bungee jump technique to force myself into the unknown and the undefined, where I am compelled to bring forward a definition equal to the declaration I have made so I can save face.

The conversational bungee jump technique is not about being 100% right or being perfect. My interest and fascination are with what my subconscious mind will deliver to answer the challenge I have created. I use the conversation to riddle myself into discovery and revelation. The conversation is my discovery portal.

Back to the "What's next?" conversation. Here are the seven levels that revealed themselves in this mental bungee jump conversation with Doug:

Level 7, at the bottom of the ladder, is survival. Over three billion people in the world live on less than $3 a day. Their focus must be on where the next meal is coming from, and how long it will sustain them. That's the "survival what's next."

Level 6 is improvement. Once the next meal is secured, people begin to ask, "What's the next improvement? How will I improve my situation? What part of my current condition can be positively improved?" That's the "improvement what's next."

Level 5 is learning. A permanent human impulse, learning comes fully alive once subsistence is resolved and living conditions are positively improved. The inquiry in this impulse is, "Where will I turn my interest to now? How will this next learning help me get ahead?" That's the "learning what's next."

Level 4 is play. A sense of relief ensues once survival needs are satisfied, conditions are improved, and learning opportunities are identified. That relief enables the nature of "What's next?" to shift into, "Where can we play and have fun? Where is the next entertainment?" That's the "entertainment what's next."

Note: For many people, life is a process of recycling through subsistence improvement, learning, and entertainment. They are unable to go beyond Level 4. For a few, "What's next?" goes beyond these endeavors to higher levels. Fewer and fewer people continue their climb up the ladder.

Level 3 is service. Here the inquiry is, "What purpose or cause will I serve next? Where can I contribute by adding value? Who will I help? How can I create new growth opportunities?" The service impulse brings about a polarity shift: the receiving is in the giving, and the benefit is in the contribution. That's the "contribution/service what's next."

Level 2 is mastery. Creating a contribution awakens the thirst and inquiry of mastery. As you seek to master the domains you serve you ask, "What's optimal? How will I master my opportunities? Where and how can I lead?" That's the "mastery what's next."

Level 1 is evolution. Evolution is the permanent impulse of the universe. When we become universe-like, we ask, "What is the next evolution and transformation? How will I help re-invent our ecosystem? What next new futures am I creating?"

My conversation with Doug continued and opened these "What's next" layers further. I embraced the trigger that Doug brought to the table, using it as a springboard to take a mental leap that resulted in the development of a new tool, a seven-rung ladder framework of "What's next?" from the bottom up:

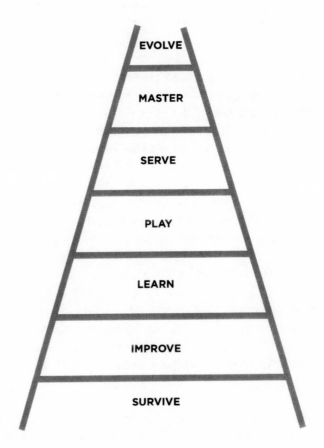

Here are two examples of how to use this seven-rung ladder framework:

Example one: as an ideation exercise in an innovation workshop.

After recounting my conversation with Doug to the innovation team, I asked the following questions:

When you think about your customers, the individuals using your products and solutions, where are they on the "What's next" ladder? Which of the seven rungs are active for them, and in what ways?

Which needs will you address? What problems can you solve better than anyone else?

What products and solutions can you develop to address these problems and needs?

How can your portfolio of products and solutions address the different levels of your customers' needs? Where do you deliver differentiated solutions to help your customers shift from one level to the next?

Example two: as a diagnostic tool during executive coaching.

I ask an executive to reflect on the issues she brings to the table and designate where each one belongs. I ask, "How would you characterize each of these topics? Are they survival, improvement, or learning issues? Or are they play issues? Perhaps you consider some to be a service/contribution inquiry, or a personal mastery examination."

By teaching executives to be diagnostic about their process and inquiry, I help them heighten their self-awareness. In turn, I am able to orient myself to the essence of their inquiries.

Simply by applying the conversational bungee jump technique, my phone call with Doug became a discovery portal through which all these new process tools and possibilities opened up.

Although you may know where you want to begin a dialogue, keep an open mind about where it leads you and what growth opportunities it might uncover. Your next conversation with a friend may provide the trigger you need to launch the innovative startup business you have not been able to get off the ground yet.

Insight:

• Conversation is a discovery portal.

Practice application:

- Become invested in your conversations. Pay attention when you speak. Believe that innovative ideas can show up in your everyday interactions.

- Apply the conversational bungee jump technique. Create riddles you are committed to solve, then come up with the solutions.

Portal 4

The Leadership Art of Recasting Mental Models

Where we discover what mental models are and why creating a new future requires building new mental models.

Though hard to believe, I probably did not touch money for the first time until just before my ninth birthday. I was born and raised in a kibbutz in Israel, where there was no such thing as pocket money. You did not need money in the kibbutz. Everything you needed was provided. In worldly terms we may have been poor, but we were the richest people on Earth: we had everything we needed. When I did touch money for the first time, someone quickly instructed me, "Wash your hands after you touch money." The message was clear: money was dirty. That was my first mental model imprint about money. Years later I would embark on a journey to update that initial mental model.

Can You Turn up the Lights?

It is late afternoon as we line up on the runway for the last flight of the day. Practicing war games makes for long, intense training days, and this is my third flight today. Yet I cannot wait to get back in the air. I am a young A4 Skyhawk pilot, and I enjoy the exhilaration of flying.

Late flights can be a beautiful experience, filled with majestic views of the setting sun. As we take off for this final flight of the day, the sun is at just the right angle to send rays of light directly into my eyes. I pull the visor down to block the glare.

Stunning. I marvel during these summer late afternoon flights while I watch the subtle color changes on the desert floor as the day comes to a close. They are beautiful, grand, almost mystical. After several passes through low valleys and some tight maneuvers, we turn back to base in a sky filled with hues of orange and pink from the setting sun. As I make the final approach, I notice that the runway lights are hard to see because they are a little dim. "Can you turn up the lights?" I ask the control tower over my radio.

"Sure," is the reply. The lights on the runway immediately brighten. "Thanks," I say. The officer in the control tower then adds, "You might want to lift your visor."

Luckily, there are only a few other pilots in the air who hear this exchange and witness my embarrassment. I smile, pull the visor up, and make a good landing.

What did I learn that afternoon?

First, embarrassment can be a good and memorable teacher. Keeping a good sense of humor helps you turn embarrassment into a helpful lesson. Second, always check yourself first: are you the cause of the dim lights? Third, the answer often is closer than you think, perhaps even literally in front of your nose, as it was in my case. Fourth, asking for help is the fastest way to get an external perspective. We all can ask others to help us turn up the lights more often.

The fifth insight that day was about mental models—specifically, how we get locked into a thinking pattern that prevents us from seeing what is right in front of us. Why did I not realize that it was my visor that made the runway look darker? At that moment I was locked into the "visor mental model," a thinking frame that distorted my interpretation of what I saw. I needed the tower officer to recognize and alert me to the fact that I was looking for the runway through the visor.

We fall into this kind of thinking pattern daily. We look at situations with a mental model that determines what we see and what we do not see. These models set the boundaries around what we believe is doable and what is not. By configuring the picture in front of us, our mental model determines whether we operate effectively or ineffectively.

Mental Models and the Games of Life

New mental models are critical for more than establishing an effective human interface with technology. As I discovered through the conversation on my flight from Houston to Seattle, technology interface is a clear case in point inside a much broader context. My work with executive teams shows that mental models play a critical role in personal growth and organizational success. My experience is that the most adaptive and resilient leaders are those who are able to recast and update their mental models quickly. Effective leaders help their people embrace new challenges and opportunities by demonstrating their own ability to evolve their mental models as necessary.

Helping people adapt and be resilient is the work of leadership. How do leaders do this work of enabling people to embrace new mental models?

As a leader, you are called first to demonstrate your own evolution, then to create the conversations that enable your teams to build and co-own the future of the organization and their own transformations inside it.

Let's address mental models. What are they? How should we think of mental models? How do they change and evolve? How have you altered the mental models you use during your life's journey?

A good place to start is to realize that you were an expert at creating and playing with new mental models by the time you completed kindergarten. As an imaginative and curious six-year-old, whether you played with dolls, ninjas or Legos, or imagined yourself as your hero or heroine, you embraced a new mental model.

At eight years old, I imagined I was Tarzan, and I learned to do the Tarzan yell. In my mind I became the master of the jungle. A couple of years later, I envisioned myself as Neil Armstrong. I put on an astronaut suit to help me imagine stepping onto the moon and "making one small step for man, and one giant leap for mankind." Today's six- and seven-year-olds practice new mental models when they play computer games.

The childhood games we played introduced us to new mental models. A mental model is what defines the rules of the game. Taking part in any game is an exercise in internalizing a new map of meaning.

The rules of checkers, for example, only work inside the mental model of how you navigate the round disks across the checkerboard. The mental model of chess necessarily is different, supporting the moves of the pawns, the rooks, the bishops, the knights, the king and the queen. The game of Snakes and Ladders, which includes an element of luck, adopts a different mental model altogether: luck and misfortune can strike you at any stage of the game. Chess, on the other hand, is a luck-free game that is won through strategic mastery.

We have all learned to embrace mental models so we could play these games. No doubt you have encountered people who approach life as a game of Snakes and Ladders, hoping to find the ladder shortcut to get ahead and struggling to avoid sliding back down a snake. Perhaps you've tried this approach yourself.

You also have encountered the checkers approach to life: being ready to sacrifice almost everything in order to get to the top of the board—the crown line—and gain greater power.

These examples of mental models are neither good nor bad, nor right or wrong. They each represent a thinking model that sets and operates within its own constraints. Just as the rules of the road are meant to enable safe passage to drivers' destinations, the rules of each mental model delineate the permitted possibilities and restrictions.

By the age of 12, you already had mastered a series of mental models. Every time you did something for the first time, you had to assimilate the map that enabled you to operate successfully within its boundaries.

In the early 2000s, when the Internet was gaining popularity rapidly, my mother was in her 70s. She had no problem assimilating the new technology required to get online and navigate. Yet I have seen other people, both older and younger, who struggle and resist integrating this technology into their lives. Being able to thrive, and not just survive, is a function of being adaptive and agile in assimilating new mental models.

One way or the other, life provides you with opportunities to experiment with transitions caused by the assimilation of new mental models. Through your experiences and interactions, you explore, inquire, and discover a variety of mental maps. Ask yourself:

- How is this mental model working?
- What results does it create?
- How does it make me feel?
- Is this the optimal mental model for me or do I need to find another?

In your youth, you likely tried a number of athletic and sport disciplines, and experienced the difference between team sports and solo sports. At age 12, I loved to play soccer and was good at it. At the same time, I excelled at cross-country distance running. Although I loved the team experience of soccer, I discovered that I had much greater control of the outcomes of distance running because the race involved just me and my body. The mental model of distance running required me to combine the strategy of the race with the capacity to push beyond my pain threshold. I mastered these requirements and became the Israeli champion for my age group. The mental model of the distance race is a configuration I lean on in the face of challenge and opportunity. The solitary focus I mastered in that sport served me well later in other areas of my life.

We all use mental models. Your beliefs and capabilities become operative inside your mental model (thinking framework). Whether you recognize or overlook opportunities is determined by your mental map.

My Meryl Moment in Toronto: Which 90% Loss Do You Prefer?

I watch and listen to interviews to find their hidden gems. Over time, I have honed the capacity to recognize them when they appear. Once I see a gem, I capture and retain it. I know it will come in handy in the future. One such gem appeared in the early 2000s during a radio interview with actress Meryl Streep. The host asked, "What do you do when you are on the set, the cameras are about to roll and you don't feel in character?"

"What a great question!" I thought. Her answer bowled me over. Without even pausing to think, and with a hearty laugh, Streep replied, "I remind myself how much they pay me and I immediately am in character." If I needed proof that money was a form of energy, Streep had just given me one.

On Sunday, September 14, 2008 I had a Meryl moment in my Toronto hotel room. Financial markets worldwide were reeling from the news of the collapse of Lehman Brothers. The company was set to file for bankruptcy on Monday morning, just as I was beginning a three-day strategy workshop with the leadership team of Hewlett-Packard Canada. There was real fear and anxiety about the world's economic stability in the air. Unless I found a way to re-direct the fear energy, external events could jeopardize the entire workshop, rendering it useless.

I don't do useless. Even though I don't get paid as much per project as Meryl Streep does, providing a "useless" service for clients doesn't work for me. All my consulting is referral-based. Projects come my way because one senior executive tells another senior executive how he or she had benefited from and enjoyed our collaboration. These executives recommend that their colleagues work with me, too. My favorite referral story involves Greg Shoemaker, the Chief Procurement Officer for Hewlett-Packard. He told his friend Rick Hughes, who held the same role at Procter & Gamble, "Hey Rick, I know how much you hate consultants. You've got to talk to Aviv. He is very different." That comment opened the door for me to a series of projects in Procter & Gamble. However, it is always up to me to deliver the promised value. The improved results that clients experience from our work together bring in the next projects. So frankly, I cannot afford to waste a precious opportunity to deliver breakthrough value to clients. With the global economy teetering on the verge of implosion, I had to think of something quickly to prevent the headline news from hijacking our session.

Fortunately, my craft is the art of conversation. I fashion discussions that enable people to get from point A to their desired point B. That is what process choreography and conversation design are about. That night, my mind was racing for a way to open Monday morning's session that would acknowledge the anxiety in the air without letting it derail our project. How could I engage the leadership team in a way that would compel them to focus on the work we were there to do?

Here's how I began our session the next morning:

"Imagine two men," I said. "One of them had $10 million in his bank account last week; the other had $100 million. Today each discovered that he had lost 90% of his money, leaving the first man with a million dollars and the second with ten million dollars. Which of these two men is facing a more challenging adjustment and why?"

After a 20-minute robust debate about which 90% loss was preferable, with good arguments on both sides of the ledger, we were ready to engage with the workshop agenda.

Cataclysmic events challenge our mental models and force us to examine how we see the world. A war, a moon landing, the assassination of a president, a global economic implosion, the loss of a loved one—these are tectonic, shattering events that compel us to see the world differently and challenge us to shift our mental models so we can continue to move forward.

Are You the Commercial Airline Captain or the Day Trader on Wall Street?

Your professional pursuits help shape your mental model. If you work on Wall Street, you must embrace the Wall Street mental model: "There are winners and losers. To get ahead, you must reduce your losses and increase your wins."

To thrive in sales, you must embrace the mental model that says, "Some will (buy), some won't (buy); you need to get through the no's to get to the sale," and the mindset that says, "When a door closes, three windows open up."

As a captain of a commercial airliner, your mental model is "safety first." Your first priority is delivering your passengers safely to the gate at your destination. Your second priority is arriving on time, and your third is creating the most comfortable experience possible for your passengers. Safety, timeliness, and comfort define your mental model as an airline pilot.

Your mindset, beliefs and attitude all permeate your mental model. Together they make up your map of meaning that defines how you see the world. Whether you choose to apply a scarcity mindset or an abundance mindset, the beliefs and attitudes it represents engender the map you configure in your head that defines your reality.

A new future cannot appear inside an old mental model. In 1994, South Africa's Truth and Reconciliation Commission was charged with abolishing the mental model that enabled apartheid. The resulting court-like restorative justice procedures introduced a conversation designed to enable what had been unimaginable prior to that process of reconciliation.

Enabling a different desired future requires the emergence of a new map of meaning (mental model). Creating a future that will release you to greater freedom, prosperity, and joy begins with changing and updating your mental map.

How do leaders introduce a new mental model?

Great leaders challenge our thinking by defying the status quo. They introduce a new map of meaning and thinking that invites us to assimilate a new perspective. They inspire us to transform our views and beliefs about our situation by showing and leading us into new ways of seeing the world.

In his first inaugural address in 1933, U.S. President Franklin D. Roosevelt (FDR) declared, "The only thing we have to fear is fear itself." This statement was a call to the nation to change its mental model. FDR knew that he had to inject a new conversation to overcome the fear and depression that threatened the country's psyche and enable the public to imagine a new and confident tomorrow. To unleash that future, FDR had to confront the anxiety of a nation, and challenge its people to envision a bold American future. That's what leaders do, and FDR rose to the occasion.

To lead is to convene conversations that recast our mental models and open possibilities previously invisible to us. Leaders facilitate the dialogue that frees people from becoming stuck in yesterday. They demonstrate how to open new doors today. Their conversations choose life, possibility, healing, and rebirth; they generate options, shape opportunities, and envision what can be.

What creates portals into the desired future?

Conversations that enable people to embrace new maps of meaning.

In the next portals I will share a series of conversations I facilitated that you can use to help your leadership teams create the desired future for your organization.

Insights:

- A mental model is the thinking framework you apply in any given situation; it is your map of the world. Beliefs and capabilities become operative, and opportunities and challenges are recognized or missed depending on your mental model.

- You cannot grow and evolve without changing your thinking models. During the journey to and through adulthood, we confront our maps of meaning, which shape our relationships with people, places, money, success, and leadership.

- New skills and endeavors can become operative only after you embrace a mental model that supports them.

- The work of a leader is to create the desired new future by helping others develop sustainable mental models that make it possible.

Portal 5

How to Scale and Speed up
by Slowing Down

*Where we apply the Air Force debrief ritual to build
a practice that can save your business and your life.*

Jen's voice is tense. She is excited about speaking with me,
and her words are positive and enthusiastic. But what I hear
underneath her story, and in the tonality of her voice, is a
huge amount of stress. Since her company's reorganization, she
no longer has P&L responsibility, though this is not the source of
her stress. Something inside her is wound tightly; the gears are
turning, but not catching, and it is not obvious to her that her
effort at finding enthusiasm is hitting a wall. She then tries even
harder to be positive about what she says. I can feel the mental
and psychological pain.

Jen is experiencing the "double microwave oven" syndrome. In
large part due to her new boss, she is cooking inside the toxic
hysteria of her workplace. Internally, Jen has become her own
microwave oven of brain reactivity, low self-esteem, resentment
and fear.

She is not alone. In fact, Jen's condition is a symptom of a
growing epidemic in the workplace that has multiple faces: inability
to adapt, punitive stress, and the breakdown of leadership presence
and organizational culture. "Workplace hysteria," a condition

in which reactivity is the mode of operation, reduces too many knowledge workers to operating at only 20 or 30 percent capacity.

Jeff Bezos, Bill Gates, the Air Force and the Law of the Tree

I am meeting with a Cisco team responsible for one of the company's fastest growing businesses. For a number of years these leaders have propelled Cisco into dramatic growth in market share. The purpose of our workshop is to develop a strategy to build the team's forward momentum.

We debrief their success so far. In pairs, they explore the following questions:
- What have we accomplished this year?
- What is working really well?
- What can we learn from our recent challenges and from our successes?

When we get back together, each pair offers the distillation of its conversations. Here are some representative comments:
- We have consistently over-delivered on our growth targets.
- We have gained market share for three consecutive years.
- We have increased our sales dramatically.
- We are building on the strength of our brand.
- We deliver superior technical knowledge.
- Our partners see us as experts in our field.
- Our teams work very hard.

The list builds as they describe their success and intensity of work. I ask the team, "Do you think your approach is sustainable? Will you be able to continue building this momentum? You already work very hard; do you think working harder will deliver the next phase of growth?"

These questions are designed to create a space for reflection and to engender awareness of the challenge and opportunity before them.

To achieve these two objectives, we first anchor ourselves in strength by focusing on what is working well and on accomplishments. That is the "Law of the Tree" in action. The tree only grows from its roots and trunk. Adult humans grow from our strengths and on the foundation of our core competence, values, and passion. These are the roots that nourish our endeavors, and lead us to grow beyond our imagined limitations.

I proceed with the next question. "Do you believe the muscle that got you to this point of success is sufficient to get you where you need to go next year?"

This conversation creates an opening for self-examination. I proceed to nudge the door still wider to suggest that this workshop is an opportunity to step back and be reflective, to help them realize what has enabled their success, and what they must do going forward, as they climb the next mountain of growth.

Just a few centuries ago, most people lived on farms or in agricultural communities. The yearly cycles created a rhythm to life, and the seasons took care of people's balance. Fall changed into winter; winter was the time to reflect before spring.

To suggest that the yearly cycles of nature resulted in a more balanced life than we experience today, I draw a picture of two equally-sized boxes that represent action and reflection.

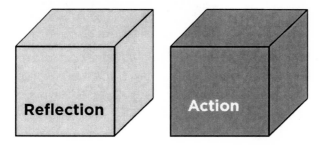

Technological breakthroughs and the onset of modernity brought with them the promise that people would have more time for leisure and for reflection. But the process of this rapid technological development caused an intriguing paradox. We are able to experience the tremendous increase in productivity and freedom that come with increased knowledge and access. We are able to do what was unimaginable just a few decades earlier. At the same time, many people feel enslaved by the pace and race of life and work.

Based on the premise that humans have the capacity to reflect, learn, and gain wisdom, we call ourselves the sapient specie. My observation, however, is that many successful teams experience a great imbalance.

"You all have been extremely successful," I point out to the team, "though it has come at a price. Stop and think for a moment. Do you see that in your 24/7 fast-paced life, you suffer the imbalances of a lot of action with little or no reflection?

"We often are not as sapient or as smart and wise as we could be because we have lost the ability to reflect, or even concentrate. In fact, we've all seen teams of very smart people applying their propensity for action in ways that produce collective stupidity and even collective disaster rather than collective wisdom."

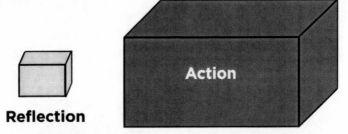

I've shown the above visual to thousands of people: a huge red box of action that leaves space only for a very small blue box of reflection. Each time, without fail, I see on people's faces the look of recognition saying, "Yes, that's me, that's what my life looks like."

We see the dangerous consequences of this imbalance all around us in multiple ways. We see individuals and organizations suffering the dangerous consequences of this imbalance in a variety of ways:

Personal Consequences	Company Consequences
Stress and anxiety	Broken communication
Burnout	Misunderstandings and conflicts
Health problems	Loss of productivity
Loss of motivation	Bad service
Loss of commitment and loyalty	System failures
Accidents	Cross-purpose work
Missed opportunities	Absenteeism
Undirected and unused energy	High turnover
Low satisfaction	Corporate ethical breakdowns

The list goes on...

I present this concept to the team and invite them to craft a new conversation. They recognize the consequences and risks of the "always on" modus operandi. This workshop conversation gives them permission to slow down. I persuade them to take this step with me into a more reflective space during the few days we are together.

"Taking time to reflect may save you and your team from many of the above negative consequences. Building a practice of reflection and debrief is vital and valuable in your proactive planning, as well as in contingent and remedial situations. You proactively avoid undesired consequences by redirecting your work. In contingent situations you use reflection to find remedial strategies and solutions."

To gain new insights, to realize and exchange learning and to build new "muscle memory," I suggest we rediscover the power of reflection.

The benefits of developing and sustaining a practice of reflection are exponential. A case in point is Bill Gates, who throughout his career insisted on taking week-long retreats to think, read and reflect, "and not do emails." Gates reported that some of his most important realizations and revelations emerged during these times of reflection, including the decision to focus on the Gates Foundation.

Another example is Jeff Bezos, founder of Amazon, who takes quarterly retreats during which he isolates himself from the world for two to three days to reflect on what is emerging on the cutting edge. This space allows Bezos to be creative and to come up with new strategic themes and directions, which he writes up as a memo to himself. These themes and ideas guide his conversations with the executive team at Amazon. Critical developments at Amazon have been instigated by Bezos's quarterly reflection retreats.

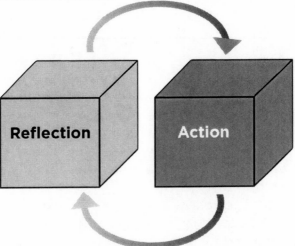

People intuitively know that their success and the intensity of their work create an imbalance they struggle to address. By introducing this mental model, and showing these visuals, I gain the team's attention and create the permission and space to balance action with reflection while we are together.

I explain the Air Force debrief ritual. "The day is not finished until we do a debrief. The Air Force rule is that an action not debriefed is a wasted action. It may have been a successful action or an unsuccessful one, but unless we debrief, we don't know what the results are. We don't know what worked well that we may need to repeat, or what did not work well, that we must learn from so we can do better next time.

"The debrief discipline is how the Israeli Air Force developed one of the best learning organizations in the world. This team has the capacity to activate these same processes and rituals right here in this workshop."

We proceed to the next conversation. The leaders form groups of three. I ask them to reflect on, and debrief, specific questions:

- What are the top behaviors that make the best performers on your team so successful?
- What are the best practices and secrets that drive your own success?

I ask them to be specific, describing concrete behaviors and practices. I coach them to ask follow-up questions, such as:

- What specifically about this behavior creates such results?
- What have you learned by working to optimize and simplify processes?
- Where have these practices and behaviors been most successful? Where have they failed? Why?
- What about this particular practice makes it "best in class?"

The team delineates the advantage created by specific best practices and behaviors. They describe developing consultative and outcome-based approaches to sales, templates to review with their teams, account planning frameworks, daily and weekly rituals, and more. They are energized to discover the wealth of knowledge available in the room.

There is immediate pragmatic and concrete value to be found in the sharing of one's practices. During the next hour, as they agree to build a practice-sharing forum that holds managers accountable to capture and share learning, I observe a sense of relief and revitalization.

That approach is how we build differentiation and unleash new futures. The Action/Reflection model creates a pivotal recognition and a need. The ensuing conversations open new possibilities and lead to an agreement to establish a learning community at work. By creating high impact learning applications and building shared accountability, such a community of practice becomes a huge differentiator.

In the following two days we address the long-term and the near-term, the strategic, and the tactical. We identify new capabilities the team must develop or bring in from the outside. We practice a series of coaching and consulting modalities the managers can use with their teams.

On the last day of the workshop, we gather for our closing circle ritual. One by one people summarize their key learning and insights, and the actions they have committed to take.

"I've realized that in order to speed up, we first need to slow down," says one senior leader. "As we slow down, we discover new opportunities to speed up and scale up. I can see now how I can be the pebble in the pond that creates the ripples of the multiplier effect."

Another leader comments that this has been the most positive and impactful experience of the many years of his professional career.

"Tell me specifically, what made it so impactful for you?" I ask.

"We were able to make the complex simple. You guided us in addressing successive horizons of the business while integrating personal introspection and a collaborative team bonding experience. You differentiated the foreground as what we do at work and the background as how we do our work together, then showed us how to evolve each one as needed. This complex integration, made simple, produced exceptional results for our team. It's almost magical how much we were able to get out of this experience."

In the next portals I will share how to build and apply these practices.

Insights:

• Adults learn best and grow from strengths. Your competence, core values and passion are the roots that nourish your development.

• The always-on, fast pace of life has fostered a breed of managers who suffer the extreme imbalances of a lot of action with little or no reflection. This makes them prone to collective stupidity, and even collective disaster, rather than to collective wisdom.

Practice application:

Ask yourself and your team:
• Do you believe the muscles that got you to this level of success are sufficient to get you where you need to go next year?

• What new capabilities must you foster to help you address the next series of opportunities?

Getting From the Bottom to the Top of the Class

Becoming a champion learner is the first competitive advantage you can develop. By "champion learner" I mean someone who brings an insatiable thirst for knowledge and an un-compromised commitment to learning, in every situation, and in every interaction.

Imagine approaching every day ready to maximize its learning opportunities. That kind of passion creates extraordinary learners who unleash radical growth that seems improbable, and that defies conventional wisdom.

I first internalized this type of focused learning in my training as an Air Force fighter pilot. I started the program at the bottom of the class. I was not your "gut pilot," one of the naturals who feels the plane right away and has an instinctive sense of how to maneuver. Flying was not second nature to me.

But what quickly did become second nature to me was learning. The Air Force debrief rule became my rule, one that I have applied daily ever since.

Embracing the idea that an un-debriefed action is a wasted action was a game-changer for me. Every day in the briefing room I reviewed what I had done well, and identified opportunities for improvement. I analyzed every maneuver and moment during the flight, and I asked others about their learning. I used the daily debrief to help me get better by maximizing the application of learning.

Although I started the program at the bottom of my class, I improved every day. People who initially performed better than me were told to leave, while I moved from one phase to the next, enhancing my performance at every stage. Thanks to the debrief rule, I finished the program second in my class, with the most dramatic rate of improvement record.

One more thing happened as a result of the fighter pilot training. I embraced and made the debrief rule my own. If it was good enough to allow me to excel in the Air Force, it was good enough to apply everywhere else. It became my Socrates credo. "The unexamined life is not worth living," declared Socrates. I decided I would never waste a day; I would debrief every day of my life.

Capturing and applying their learning is the mark of highly successful professionals. They improve and optimize what they do by distilling and applying actionable insights from their own experiences and those of other people. By doing so, they become champion learners.

Champion learners approach learning opportunities with curiosity and interest. They make the most out of a situation through focus and the application of their insights. They are not defensive in the face of learning; they do not mind who or what is the source of their learning, and they do not let pride stand in the way of making themselves better performers and leaders. Their sole interest is to grow and become better, and to help their people thrive. They embrace learning that will support improvement and growth.

Recall your favorite learning experience. Perhaps it was the first day of high school or college. Remember how excited and energized you were. Perhaps you experienced that energy each time you stepped into the class of your favorite professor, who had a magical way of engaging you and stimulating your learning. Participating in that class was so fascinating that during those sessions there was nothing else in the whole world, only the discussions in the classroom with your teacher.

Adopting the debrief practice unleashes the power of fully engaged learning. It grabs more than your brain; it engages you totally, captures your imagination and inspires your ability to learn. It rewires every cell in your body.

Now imagine that such a state of captivated engagement is the order of the day for you, and that you bring this energized focus to all that you do. Imagine that you inspire others to become champion learners as well, simply by sharing the power of the debrief ritual.

Where do we see examples of champion learning behaviors? Pioneering entrepreneurs, great actors and artists, champion athletes, and the best leaders all embrace the learning ethos that uses every opportunity to engage in the refinement of their mastery. What differentiates them is their focus on learning and improving. They approach life as a learning experience with the credo that "to live is to always be learning and evolving." They never stop refining their craft; they are always moving forward to create radical new futures.

Building the Forensic Debrief Practice
to Enter the Learning Zone

In most of our strategy and innovation workshops with executive teams, I begin by asking participants to reflect on and capture their learning from recent successes and challenges. To facilitate the entry into the learning zone, I ask them to be forensic about their learning. By forensic I mean being specific, concrete, and penetratingly substantive.

There are a number of reasons why a high impact workshop must begin by having attendees consciously enter and embrace the learning zone. First, unlocking participants' learning triggers a huge growth potential.

Second, the breakthrough we are working to create requires the executives to raise the authenticity bar by engaging at a high level of intensity.

Third, quickly evolving and transforming ourselves requires us to generate the learning that is possible only by unleashing the necessary brain chemistry.

As a result, we get where we are going faster, more effectively, and in better shape than we would have otherwise.

Let's start with an example of a statement that is common among people who have not entered the learning zone: "Things are tough; we have a lot of challenges." This mindset clearly does not trigger the brain's creativity or the discovery that facilitates engagement. Unless executives turn this perspective around immediately, they will miss the growth opportunity that is possible in their first twenty minutes with me.

Why doesn't the above statement qualify as learning? First, saying "things are tough" adds no new information about the situation. Second, do you really believe that your corporate career and challenges rise to the level of tough? Before you answer, try this reality check: take a look at the news. There are some really hard-hitting stories in the headlines this week. Compared to those, do you still feel that your career challenges are tough?

The third and most important reason why saying "things are

tough" does not qualify as learning is this: instead of lamenting your situation, consider the reality that if everything were to go smoothly by itself, you would have no opportunity for growth, and a diminished or no role in your organization. The reason you have a job is that there are problems to be solved, and clients and stakeholders who require your help. As an executive and a manager, you are paid to solve complex problems. So if you feel that things are tough at work, say, "Thank you," and embrace the opportunities that complex challenges offer.

Now let's turn to an example of what does qualify as learning, and how you can succeed in the first twenty minutes of debrief in my workshop. Here is what one executive said during a recent strategy event: "I've realized that I resisted the changes in our organization because I was afraid to lose the sense of autonomy and control I had enjoyed, and because I was worried that I was not going to be able to replicate my recent success in this new situation. Instead, I found that the organizational changes have pushed me into a whole new learning curve that has totally energized and invigorated me and my team. My breakthrough insight is that the fastest growth occurs when I embrace what I most fear and resist."

With that statement, this executive got everyone's attention. It was raw and authentic, and it embodied the learning we all needed.

Here is another example of failing to enter the learning zone by throwing out a thought or belief that doesn't qualify as true learning: "We have a problem with collaboration. We need to collaborate more."

Really? Why do you need to collaborate more?

My experience with executive teams has taught me that the collaboration story can serve as a great camouflage for the true issue that people don't want to recognize and refuse to discuss. Collaboration becomes a smoke screen they easily can hide behind.

Let's look at a second example of meaningful learning shared in the first twenty minutes of a strategy workshop by an insightful executive: "By asking team members to articulate clearly what they need in order to succeed, and by following their answers with a second and third, and at times even a fifth "Why?" we are able to build a deep understanding of the relevant issues. Such profound awareness enables us to accelerate our alignment significantly and improve the quality of our interactions by converting issues into clear proposals and solutions. My learning is that this process requires discipline, and the readiness to engage at high levels of intensity. We further accelerate this conversation by asking people to formulate clear and concrete requests and proposals."

This executive's insight stopped us in our tracks. He got our attention by pointing to the prevalent blind spot: too often collaboration is a peripheral and/or displaced issue that camouflages the real need and masquerades as the issue at hand. Instead, the executive proposed that organizational and team effectiveness require us to make investments in each other. We build more robust and resilient teams that perform at a much higher level by inquiring deeply, and by going out of our way to find out how we can help people on our team succeed.

What enables a new future to find us?

The debrief practice that brings forward insights and activates breakthrough learning is where a new future begins.

Insights:

• An action that is not debriefed is a wasted action.

• Champion learners are not defensive. They don't let pride stand in the way of making themselves better performers and leaders. Their sole interest is to become better, and to refine their craft.

Practice application:

- Develop for yourself and with your team a cadence of daily, weekly and monthly debriefs. Identify what is working well, and how specifically you are achieving your best results. Define concrete actions and behaviors you will implement. Continue to debrief.

Escape the Monty Syndrome: Are You Productive or Just Busy?

There is one more conversation I introduce when we look at the action and reflection visual. I ask managers, "Do you realize that engaging in nonstop activity can be a form of addiction, a 'busyness' addiction?"

You might ask, "What is a busyness addiction?"

You see and experience it yourself every time you confuse "urgent" with "important," or when you mistake being "busy" for being "productive."

Ask yourself these questions: Are you constantly busy? Do you allow yourself to fall into the "activity trap" by moving from urgency to urgency to create never-ending busyness, to the point that it has become your second nature?

Is "being busy" an identity, or even a status symbol for you?

I see too many people who reinforce their sense of self-importance or feel they impress others by staying obsessively busy. They end up filling their lives with an excessive amount of urgent but unimportant stuff.

The addiction to being constantly occupied by something that feels urgent often is triggered by an unhealthy self-esteem. Low self-esteem creates a distorted self-view. It builds in a person the sense of "as long as I am busy, I am included. I am in on what is happening and I am important."

Monty was a manager with low self-esteem, despite the fact that he was a talented engineer with a creative mind. He developed a habit of always walking fast because he believed it communicated to others that he was a very busy man who always was on his way to something important. His mental model was that successful people are busy people. Therefore, he thought that being constantly on the move earned him respect from his peers and superiors because they could see he was successful.

Through hard work, applying his talent and creativity and years of dedication, Monty climbed the corporate ladder to the level of Vice President. Yet he continued to credit his rise through the ranks to his hard work, and he believed that everyone else noticed he was always focused on a mission and was not wasting time.

Some years later Monty lost his job. He was in shock. What would he do now?

Monty remained very busy. He created lists of things he needed to do, and he worked on his list. For 34 years his identity had been built on how busy he appeared at work. Suddenly, there was no one waiting on his every move. Instead, there was a complete void which he filled by frantically trying to be as busy as he used to be at work. Only now his family was his audience.

Monty made two mistakes. First, he did not recognize that his earlier success arose from his engineering and creative talents. Second, when he became a manager, he distanced himself from those strengths and focused on being perceived as a busy guy with urgent things on his plate. He mistakenly believed, based on his mental model of success, that his never ending active busyness was responsible for his achievements.

Losing his job punctured Monty's self-esteem, and he was left without anyone to impress with his prodigious level of energy. Unable to find a constructive outlet, his life began to unravel. His children became more distant emotionally, his marriage was in a crisis, and his health began to suffer.

Can you relate to Monty's story?

Do you feel you have to be constantly busy? Are you caught inside the activity trap? Or do you give yourself permission to step back before the trap turns into a busyness addiction?

Do you feel uneasy if you are not constantly occupied with something? Or are you able to enjoy where you are, even if you are not doing something? Do you give yourself permission to be reflective at work and in your life?

Consider this thought: to be great, you must let go of some of the good, so the great can find you. While it may feel invigorating to be busy, you cannot be productive when the activities that occupy your time have no consequence for you, are not aligned to the future you hope to create, and do not move you closer to living your purpose. To create a compelling future, you must make space for new and inspiring conversations so that fresh possibilities can find you.

Although most people understand the need to prioritize, stepping back from the activity trap and the busyness addiction requires going beyond organizing your day. It is about reclaiming your life, discovering what is important to you, and learning how to create new ways of being and doing that make a difference.

Insight:

• The activity trap produces a false sense of focus and is an expression of low self-esteem. Productive and effective living is built upon the foundation of a healthy self-esteem.

Practice application:

Escape the self-inflicting blind spot of the activity trap:

- Plan to have 10-20 minutes at the start of every day to reflect and focus on the two or three most important goals for you today.

- Leave yourself notes in your car, office, study and on your screen saver to help you break out of the activity trap. Here are some ideas you can use until you create your own:
    o "Is what I am doing now important?"
    o "Relax and take a deep breath."
    o "Enjoy, be present."
    o "What is most important for me now?"
    o "This, too, shall pass."

- Instead of treating every day as a marathon, act as if it is a series of sprints. Get up or step back every 45-60 minutes to take a moment. Take a deep breath; enjoy the view and what you do.

- Ask yourself regularly, "Am I focused on the most vital task or activity? Is there something better, more important and more energizing for me to do?"

- Allow an unplanned moment every day. For example, have a spontaneous conversation, engage in an act of kindness, express thanks and appreciation.

Practicing Level Four Listening on the Path to a Billion Dollars

We begin a strategy workshop with the leadership team of an early-stage company in Silicon Valley. The strong business acumen of each of these 16 executives has enabled them to experience success and address challenges and setbacks in their previous roles and companies. They have joined this company hoping it would lead to their next big success.

Ever since the company's IPO 18 months ago, life has been a whirlwind as the team gained traction in its market and generated a 40% growth in revenue.

The executives now want to turbo charge their growth and create a path to a billion dollars in annual revenue. How to achieve this growth is the question we are here to answer.

To design this team's conversation, I first must create a new awareness. I do this by using the action/reflection visual shown earlier.

In this case, however, I use a variation of a question I often ask other teams: "You have been very successful. Do you believe you can achieve the next level of growth and quadruple the company's revenue by working harder and doing more of what you are doing? Or do you believe that climbing this next mountain requires you to do things differently, build new 'muscles,' and leverage new ways of working?"

These are reflection questions for each executive to consider. Can you achieve the next level of success by doing more of what you have done and working harder, or must you retool and apply a new muscle to the task at hand?

To cultivate a fertile soil for insight and prepare the space for a conversation about the future, I ask the executives to consider the answers to a series of questions. They are questions you can ask yourself as you work to retool and build the space for your own future exploration:

- What are your most exciting achievements? What enabled you to create these successes?
- What was the happiest, most enjoyable day at work for you in recent months? What made this day special?
- As you reflect on and think about the best performers on your team, what are the top five behaviors that make them successful?
- What are the key practices driving your success as a leader?

Then I tell them, "Now, one more task before I let you go into your exploration. I want you to give each other a new experience by practicing Level Four listening as you discuss these questions. This will allow you to reflect and enter a truly insightful conversation."

What is Level Four listening?

To answer that question, consider first listening Levels One, Two and Three.

At **Level One listening**, you pay little attention to the words you hear. For example, during a conference call you multi-task and let the call recede into the background. You read your emails, work on a document and glance at another screen to monitor the news. While you hear the words in the background, you are not engaged in deciphering their meaning. The call comes into the foreground only when your name is mentioned, at which point you immediately shift into Level Two. At Level One listening you are largely absent from the conversation and cannot make any meaningful response. This is an insufficient and non-productive level of engagement.

At **Level Two listening**, you think about what people say, and you decipher or judge the context of what is being said according to what these words mean to you. You are primarily in a cerebral engagement at this level of listening, formulating your next question and possible response. For example, attorneys apply this form of listening in court, where the rule is to ask only questions for which you already know the answers. Level Two listening is a targeted listening that helps you steer the discussion and negotiate specific outcomes.

Level Three listening brings a new depth to the interaction. You go beyond merely listening for the meaning of words; you also filter and process the emotions and feelings behind what people say. This engagement implies you are involving a limbic process, not just a cerebral one. The limbic brain activates the functioning of emotion, motivation, and the process of social behavior. It is the part of the brain that reads the other person and adapts to enable emotional connection.

Level Four listening, also called "listening with presence," embodies the true meaning of "I am all ears." At this level, you listen to the whole person with every cell in your body. Such listening is an art, a skill, and a discipline. Like other skills, it requires self-control and practice. Listening at Level Four is an intense process because you can be fully present only when you concentrate your attention to the exclusion of all else. This form of listening can cause profound healing. The act of being fully witnessed and heard can be a transformative process for each person in the conversation.

Four Levels of Listening

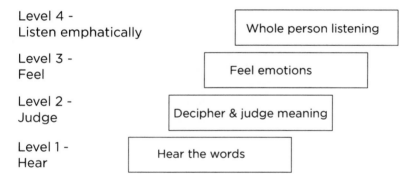

Level 4 - Listen emphatically — Whole person listening

Level 3 - Feel — Feel emotions

Level 2 - Judge — Decipher & judge meaning

Level 1 - Hear — Hear the words

I ask the team to step up to Level Four listening, to discover this way of listening empathetically and practice this new listening muscle. I ask that they give themselves permission to relax into the discovery of listening with their full presence.

When they return from the exercise, the executives look fresh and revitalized. As you listen empathically and with presence, the latent energy potential that had been held back in you, in the other person, and in the environment, is released, making you feel and look different.

Level Four listening is a radical idea that works. Not only does it open new conversation portals, it also creates a profound cosmetic treatment. Facial skin is highly sensitive to the energetic quality of your conversation. Listening with presence will change the texture of your skin—a novel concept to consider.

Insight:

• Listening with presence requires discipline. It has transformative power for both the listener and the person speaking.

Practice application:

Here are 10 tips to help you learn to engage in Level Four listening:

1. Clear out the clutter and eliminate distractions in the meeting environment. Complete open projects; stay away from the phone; silence cell phones and online devices. Look around you and redesign, or remove, what distracts you from listening so you can stay focused on the conversation.

2. Take a series of deep breaths before you begin a conversation. A deep breath is an energetic way of saying, "I am making a space for something new to happen." You replenish your brain by taking in fresh oxygen.

3. Relax any tension in your shoulders, neck or posture.

4. Focus on your value for the other person, and what you want for yourself and for the relationship. Be centered in why you want and need to move into Level Four listening.

5. Ask open-ended questions, such as, "What do you think?"

Practice application (continued):

6. Allow for silence. When the person stops speaking, count quietly in your head to three before you respond. Don't finish sentences or rush to fill in the silence with another question. The moment of quiet allows you both to move from a cerebral to a limbic process, and to bring into the conversation what otherwise would stay below the surface.

7. Write down key words. Jotting an occasional word, fact, or number can help you improve retention and remain focused on the speaker's main themes.

8. As you listen, refrain from making mental comparisons with your own experience. Discipline yourself to not engage with any comparison.

9. Do not form a response, or begin to plan what you will say next, while the other person is speaking.

10. Paraphrase. It helps you stay alert and engaged, and lets the speaker know you are listening with interest, understanding, and empathy. By paraphrasing you validate understanding and can clarify what is misunderstood. Lead with: "What I heard you say is that ..." or "So you are saying that..."

Portal 6

The Art and Science of Creating Breakthroughs

Where we explore the power of your Control Field and the virtuous cycle that creates breakthroughs.

D o you remember playing with a magnifying glass as a child, directing the sun's rays to focus on a piece of paper until it caught fire? The magnifying glass concentrated the rays, generating enough energy and heat to change the state of the paper. In the same way, a ritual is a process that helps you change your state by sharpening and magnifying your focus. In our workshops we begin the day with a morning reflection and close the day with a debrief. These simple rituals help the group center itself, harvest meaning and build significance into the team's work.

Your Control and Influence Fields

The power of a simple model and framework-based conversations can be seen in the story of the rapidly growing early stage company in Silicon Valley in Portal 5.

We started that workshop by reflecting on, and learning from, the successes and challenges experienced by the team, and we practiced Level Four listening to bring forward latent insights.

When the executives saw the visual of the big red "action" box crowding out the very small blue "reflection" box, they had an epiphany. That framework evokes intuitive realizations and facilitates the discovery that leads to application. The action/reflection visual mirrors people's busy lives and helps them see the risk inherent in being locked into the activity trap. It also demonstrates how this imbalance dramatically diminishes their impact.

This insight is liberating. People realize that they have the power to take control and influence their environment, that they are not victims of forces they cannot help to shape. At this point I introduced a new visual to trigger the next conversation breakthrough, the Control and Influence (C.I.) Fields image:

The Control and Influence Fields

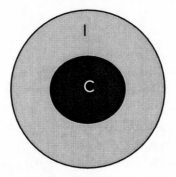

In my world there are three fields. The inner circle, labeled the C-Field, represents areas of my life that are within my control. In the outer sphere, the I-Field, are the aspects of my life in which I have varying degrees of influence but which I do not control. Outside those two circles is the rest of the world, where I have neither control nor recognizable influence.

It is the same for you. You also have a C-Field that includes the aspects of your life that you control. It includes your decisions, responses and actions, how you manage your time, and the way you organize your immediate priorities and environment.

I have two objectives in presenting the visual of the C.I. Fields early in our strategy workshop.

First, I want the executives to internalize this mental model so it engenders a sense of urgency that causes them to reclaim their Control Field and encourages them to take responsibility for developing focus and self-mastery. I seek to raise their awareness that in the C-Field they have the power to shape their experience, and to boost their confidence to exercise that power.

As the discussion evolves, the executives begin to distinguish the elements in their C-Field from those in their I-Field. That is the point of framework-based conversations. They create a structure that accelerates insights. The C-Field conversation helps people recognize that when they take time for reflection, they have the power to choose in which activities they engage. They can opt out of becoming victims of the activity trap.

Highly effective people guard their C-Field as if it were their personal nuclear power station. They build their impact and accelerate their results by first working from inside it. Then they expand it by increasing their leverage in their Influence Field.

Insight:

• To increase your leverage and influence, learn to focus on and work from inside your Control Field.

The Three Hour Rule

Jerry is one of the top sales managers for his company. The Three Hour Rule is a C-Field story he shared when I discussed the C.I. Fields with his team during a workshop.

"In 2003 I went to work one morning and found that I had 16 phone messages and a pile of emails in my inbox. Sitting quietly for a moment to reflect on this situation, I quickly realized that reacting to all those messages would keep me busy for the next three days, even if no further messages came through.

"It was clear that I would be unable to get to the day's most important objectives if I allowed myself to be managed by my inbox. So I decided to ignore the messages for the first three hours. Instead I focused on the few vital tasks I needed to accomplish that day.

"Something powerful happened as a result of this decision. Everything worked extremely well. I felt as though I was in a beam of focus that made me highly effective in achieving my objectives and tasks. This experience was an epiphany: I realized that I had the power to shut out the noise and focus on the most important tasks. That day, I decided to make this 'three-hour rule' part of my daily routine.

"I spend the first three hours of every morning focusing on the vital few things I have chosen for that day. Each evening before I leave work, I clear my desk and list the vital few tasks I will focus on the following morning. I follow this discipline religiously. This one decision and discipline has helped me consistently exceed my goals despite demanding and chaotic market environments."

By choosing to focus the first three hours of every day exclusively on his top priorities in his C-Field, Jerry proceeded to create breakthrough success.

The Metaphysics of a Strategy Workshop

In a strategy workshop we seek to create the efficacy of now. After first explaining the concept of the C.I. Fields to the leadership team, I proceed to address the challenge of the moment. Here is how I describe the efficacy of now: "My second objective in drawing the visual of the C.I. Fields is that I am going to ask you—actually, I will plead with you—to stay in our collective C-Field for the next few days as we work to create the future of your organization.

"The metaphysics of a strategy workshop like this one is that we create a field of power. It is real. I have experienced it many times, and so have you. Our collective focus, creativity and vision generate the energy potential that results in an actual field of power present in the room.

"Where is this field of power?

"The power aggregates in our collective Control and Influence Fields. As long as we work inside these fields, we are building our power. The moment we step out of the C.I. Fields by talking about what people who are not in the room should do, we dilute our focus. As a result, the power leaks out and we lose the intensity we have built. If you are sensitive, you will feel this sensation physically, and recognize the energy drop when we puncture the C.I. Fields.

"My request is for you to practice raising your awareness of the C.I. Fields. Throughout the workshop I will hold you accountable for maintaining the practice and integrity of focusing on the C.I. Fields regardless of the topic of discussion.

"How do we make sure we are staying in the C.I. Fields? By taking responsibility and stepping up to own what is ours.

"As we move through the next few days, I am going to keep this visual in sight so that as you describe your ideas, strategic proposals and initiatives, we can refer to it as we determine whether what you are describing is inside our C-Field. The Control Field contains a specific set of conversations; the Influence Field contains a different set. Then there are conversations that dilute our power because they are outside both the Control and the Influence Fields.

"How do you weaken your power by diluting your C-Field?

"Blaming others, complaining about what someone else should do, and seeing yourself as a victim of events weakens your C-Field. Becoming preoccupied with matters you have no influence over and cannot control provides zero return on your efforts, dispenses time and energy into something that creates no impact, and weakens your C-Field.

"To realize your power to make a difference, concentrate on areas within your Control Field. Investing your precious resources and time in areas outside your control, or where your influence is marginal, is detrimental."

Insights:

- You lead by first becoming clear about what is in your control, and then by expanding your spheres of influence.

- A leadership team for a function, a business unit or a company has specific control points. Use those levers to influence and to create value.

Practice application:

Create your Control Field map. Write down everything that is inside your C-Field and then everything that is part of your I-Field.

For instance, my C-Field contains:

- The words I speak
- What I write
- My responses
- What I listen to
- What I eat
- When I go to sleep
- What I read
- Conversations I start
- The priorities I set
- What I choose to support
- What I choose to focus on in the first 90 minutes of the day

You get the idea.

Practice application (continued):

Then list everything that is part of your Influence Field. For example:

- You cannot control your congressional representative or senator, but you have some degree of influence. You control whether you write a letter, as well as what it says.

- You do not control your boss and her priorities, yet you can influence her priorities.

- You have significant influence on the collaboration and relationships you develop with peers but you do not control their level of engagement.

- You do not control your stakeholders' Net Promoter Score (NPS), but you influence the score because you have control over your input and over how you frame your engagement.

Hold a Control Field Day! Spend a day focused on staying inside your Control Field. When you step out of it (because you will), step back in. You might find it helpful to tell people around you that you are practicing a new discipline. Look at everything you do in your life and ask, "Is this what I am choosing to now do?"

If committing to this exercise for a full day seems insurmountable, start with an hour, say, the first hour or the first three hours of the day.

Creating Breakthroughs by Escaping Conventional Thinking

Defining conversation as the currency of work is a pivotal realization and a game-changer. If you are having the same conversation you had last year, you will remain exactly where you are now.

To arrive at a new and better place, you first must change the conversation. A new future emerges when you change the conversation you begin today. It is like flipping a switch: the light goes on.

Now we are ready. To begin a new conversation, I ask the team to bring forward big thinking.

We contrast big thinking and conventional thinking in terms of their consequences. Whereas conventional thinking creates a vicious cycle that produces a doom loop, big thinking creates a virtuous cycle that produces the breakthrough loop.

Conventional thinking ⟶ **vicious cycle** ⟶ **doom loop**

Big thinking ⟶ **virtuous cycle** ⟶ **breakthrough loop**

I was introduced to the idea of the doom loop and the breakthrough loop by Alan Weiss, the author of *Million Dollar Consulting*. Let's explore these two different cycles.

Conventional thinking is first about structure and role. It begins with the current state and it focuses on obstacles which then block the momentum and produce the doom loop.

Doom Loop

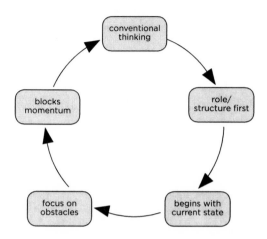

Big thinking is first about value. It begins with the future state and it focuses on opportunities, which create the regenerative momentum that produces the breakthrough loop.

Breakthrough Loop

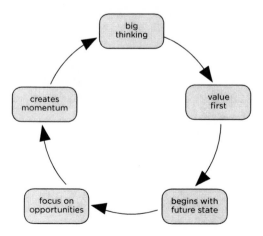

To create new conversations, we need to pivot from structure-first thinking to a value-first mindset. By beginning with the future state instead of the current state and focusing on opportunities rather than on obstacles, we build momentum rather than block it.

In the old industrial organization, the structure defined the work, which defined the value created. This mental model is the legacy mindset that governs conventional thinking in many businesses today.

This old approach holds that to understand your role, you first must understand the structure of the organization, because your responsibilities and the work you do are defined by it. The opportunities that arise and the value you create are constrained by what your structure-determined role permits you to do.

Governmental agencies are a case in point. They are bureaucratic organizations that move slowly and are unable to adapt quickly in response to new opportunities and needs.

In the conventional thinking model, my role is defined by my job. If I am assigned to do A, B and C, I need not be concerned with E, F and G; they are someone else's responsibilities. Anything outside of my job description is not for me to worry about.

Consider an organization where people focus merely on the part of the process they own, as outlined in their job descriptions. They do not care what occurs before or after. Their job is to complete their assigned tasks, not to enable the whole system to fulfill its purpose by serving its customers.

You have met this mindset in hotels, in restaurants, and other service-related organizations, where just one experience was enough for you to vow never to return.

You and I can fill a book with bad customer experiences caused by small-minded people who said it was not their job to help you solve your problem. Further, they did not offer to find someone who could help you.

How long can an organization survive when its primary orientation is to its own structure instead of to creating value for the people it is meant to serve?

Evidence strongly indicates that bureaucratic, structure-first organizational systems in the private sector as well as in government must transform or they will die by being replaced or automated out of existence.

Value-defined Work and the New Paradigm

To facilitate the shift from a structure-first to a value-first mindset, I show a visual that illustrates the pivot from the old mental model to the new way of thinking about work and organizations.

In 20th century organizations, the prevailing mental model was structure defines work and work defines value.

**Old approach: structure defined the work;
work defined the value**

When consistency and predictability were the top requirements, this industrial mindset had its merits. When the need shifted, however, and value was redefined, this organizational system was very slow to reorient itself to new needs and opportunities. In fact, it often continued to produce work that no longer had value. Think of the reports no one reads, or tools that are obsolete, or parts of appliances that no one needs any longer, or products that are unused.

This was the old model in which people performed a job, whether it served a purpose or not. The orientation was to serve the structure and the group itself, not to serve a client. Often this orientation led the organization to grow as an objective unto itself, rather than in the context of serving its clients. When structure comes first, the preservation of the system trumps the purpose it was meant to serve. Instead of preserving the system, this mindset usually hastens its decline and demise.

The new model redefines work by reversing the flow to put value first. Its mindset is that the work you do is defined by the value you create, not by your role.

The reframing of the mental model enables the shift from work defined by structure to work defined by the opportunity to serve and contribute value.

**New approach: value defines the work;
the work defines the structure**

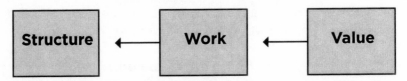

Imagine an adaptive, agile organization where the opportunities to create value and serve customers define the work employees do and how the work is organized. This approach requires a service-focused operating model, rather than one anchored in functional silos.

A great example of value-centered work can be seen in startup companies in which anyone can work on anything at any given moment, if that is what is needed to serve a perceived opportunity.

The entertainment industry is another case in point: the business model drives ad hoc teams. These teams form and organize to address the opportunity of a new movie, and they dissolve at the end of production. When a new opportunity presents itself, a different team will come together to address its needs.

When value comes first, the flow changes and instigates an agile approach to work. It changes the conversations that occur and guides the way people approach their activities. As opportunities continue to emerge and evolve, so too does the nature of the work necessary to serve the new needs. The new work informs managers how to reorganize the structure and deliver the value in the most efficient way possible.

For instance, the majority of the work I do in my consulting today is different from the work I did last year or three years ago. Why? I continuously evolve in order to provide value that meets or exceeds my clients' emergent needs.

During a meeting with a leadership team in one of the largest oil and gas companies in the world, I introduce the new flow of work that results from the shift from a structure-first to a value-first mindset. To spark a new conversation by provoking and stimulating the discussion, I push this reframing mental model all the way to the extreme end of the continuum:

"To internalize the value-first thinking, try this thought experiment. Imagine an organization where people have no job descriptions. They simply come to work every day to discover where the greatest need is, and how the most compelling opportunity to serve can find them."

To even imagine this scenario is an obvious stretch for the executives. Theirs is a company in which safety comes first. Too many changes at the same time can create dynamics that feel unsafe, depending on the mental model you operate in.

Why do I introduce this reframed mental model and thought experiment?

I am not proposing that we do away with roles and responsibilities or that we actually eliminate governance and accountability structures. I put this imaginary thought experiment in front of this leadership team to provoke a series of new conversations about how they approach their roles as leaders. The new conversations we develop help us create value-first empowered thinking that builds new leverage as we move into the discussion about strategy, execution and organizational effectiveness.

Insight:

• To lead the transformation of an organization, shift
  from work defined by structure to work defined by
  opportunities to serve and create value.

Practice application:

• Ask the people you lead, "What are you working on?"
  Listen carefully. Do they describe activities defined by
  role, or do they describe the outcomes and the value
  they produce?

What else must change when work is defined by the opportunity
to contribute rather than by structure and role?

As the opportunities to contribute become the catalyst
influencing how we prioritize our work, a new flow unleashes
the emergent capacity of an organization to self-organize.

How do people self-organize?

By engaging in intelligent conversations that map
opportunities and needs. They then develop a way to address
these emergent opportunities.

I will share some concrete examples in the next portals. But
first let's explore another reframe.

Portal 7

Begin With the Future

Where we develop the outcomes mindset and discover the power of three horizons thinking.

A great rabbi once said, "We tell stories to our children to put them to sleep. We tell stories to adults to wake them up."

Inputs, Outcomes, and Reclaiming a Life

Sanjay scheduled a call with me to discuss his business objectives for the coming year. He had identified a number of goals.

"Where would you like to begin?" I ask.

"I really want to speak more at big conferences," he replies.

"Why is speaking important to you?"

"For a few reasons: I want to be seen. I want to develop relationships with other leaders in our space. And I want bragging rights with my peers."

"Why do you want to be seen?"

"It would build up my identity. Also it would boost my ego."

"Why are those things important?" I ask further.

Sanjay thinks for a moment before speaking. "You know, this

past year at work has been tough. I've had a lot of people on my back. I need to regain control of my time. Renew myself. Feel better about myself."

"I understand, which is why I'm concerned that your focus is displaced. You're targeting INPUTS instead of OUTCOMES. Speaking at a conference is an input. What's the outcome that speaking at a conference will help you achieve?"

"I'm not sure. Give me examples of possible outcomes."

"Building your personal brand is one outcome. Being recognized as a thought leader is another. Getting on a prospect's radar and acquiring new business are outcomes. Building on these results to increase your portfolio of responsibilities can be an outcome. All those are possible outcomes from speaking. But... you can get those outcomes in other ways. For instance, you can build your personal brand, gain recognition, and get on a prospect's radar by writing and publishing articles."

"I see what you mean, Aviv. Speaking isn't the only way to get what I want."

"Exactly. If you start by defining the outcome you want most, you'll be able to identify more options that will help you achieve that outcome."

After a quiet contemplative moment, Sanjay asks, "Do you have another example?"

"You're an executive VP. In the past 12 months have you felt in control of your own time?"

"No way. I feel that I have been reacting to other people's agendas and priorities. I have been locked in a loop and stressed. I couldn't do what I wanted to do."

"You haven't had a life?"

"Exactly," Sanjay says with a sigh.

"Would you like a life? Would you like to reclaim your life?"

"You bet!"

"So, for you, 'having a life' would be an outcome. That's where you start. Here, then, is the question to explore: what must you do to reclaim your life?"

Sanjay quickly internalizes this reframed focus and the question I put to him. "Instead of being reactive, I need to be proactive," he says.

"To gain a sense of control, you must operate according to your priorities."

"That's right."

"You also must devise a work schedule and cadence that afford you breathing space. That's how you get your life back. You block out the discretionary time you need and you organize your activities around these windows. When you create some space, your life finds you. You make room to observe, to read, to reflect, to write. Oh, and space to enjoy."

Insight:

• First clarify your desired outcomes. Then explore what inputs can help you achieve them.

How can you create the future?

Formulating the outcomes you want is a good place to begin. Say you want to experience your best year yet. To do so, you begin by creating a picture of what "your best year" looks and feels like.

Here are a few more "outcomes framing" questions:
• What future do you want to create?
• What will success look like?
• What will these successes enable you to do?
• When you look back three years from now, what will make you especially proud and happy?

Too often our tendency is to begin a discussion by describing inputs and activities. As my conversation with Sanjay demonstrates, you unleash the power of outcomes-focused thinking by reversing the order. The result is actionable insights.

After articulating clearly your desired outcomes, you develop the input conversation by asking what is needed and what inputs are essential to achieve the outcomes you seek. The inputs conversation is designed to determine which activities, enabling efforts, and investments will be most effective.

Practice application:

- Create a list of personal and professional outcomes
  you want to achieve in the next 12 months. Then,
  work backwards from each goal to identify the inputs
  necessary to help you reach it. Also consider what you
  must eliminate to free up space for your desired future.

Tip: Creating an "ideal client list" is an input. Acquiring
ten great clients is an outcome.

When you ask team members, "What are you working
on?" teach them to answer by first framing the outcomes,
then the "inputs" (the work) they must do to achieve
those results.

From Frankfurt to Palo Alto, the Three Horizons

We are at the top floor of the Lufthansa office building at the
Frankfurt airport. From that vantage point we easily see the
planes approaching the runway to land. A behemoth Airbus
380 approaches as we prepare to kick-start our workshop.
There is something beautiful, even graceful in this huge plane
coming into landing. Moments later, another Lufthansa A380
takes off with extraordinary power. There is our metaphor. A
tremendous amount of work and the efforts of many dedicated
professionals have enabled this A380 to take off with some 850
passengers. It represents an astonishing feat of orchestrated
coordination, timeliness, and management that observers
almost take for granted.

Around the conference table are 12 directors, vice presi-
dents, and the Senior Vice President leading this team charged
with building a new Lufthansa subsidiary. The charter from the
company's board is defined on the basis of a business case,
establishing the expected results from the new subsidiary. The

task is to build global business services for the Lufthansa group of companies.

My brief is to facilitate the launch of the new organization by leading the workshop process. "We too must develop takeoff velocity if we are to achieve our goal. In our case, the propulsion engine will be generated by a clear sense of purpose and the vision we are here to paint," I propose.

We embark on our first morning in this conference room before moving to the beautiful Lufthansa training center for the next two days. Using the background scenery to inform the analogies and metaphors used during the workshops helps. I reflect on the importance of forward visibility in flight and proceed to make the implicit explicit: "Every flight begins by specifying the desired destination. We cannot begin to plan our flight without first being clear about our direction and where we will land."

The flight narrative provides an easy segue to discuss the Three Horizons thinking frame. "A flight includes the departure and the takeoff, the flight route to the destination, and the landing and arrival. In business we address a longer time horizon than we do in flight planning, and we must reflect on three horizons." I project the Three Horizon visual to anchor the conversation.

Three Horizons

Horizon One	Horizon Two	Horizon Three
Here and now	The space in the middle	The future

Here we shape the landscape

Horizon One (H1) represents the near term, and the here and now. Horizon Three (H3) is the future to which we aspire. Horizon Two (H2) is the space in the middle that represents where we do the work that enables our desired future by going beyond just running the business (H1).

One of the most-told Silicon Valley stories is about the renowned Xerox PARC (Palo Alto Research Center). In the 1970s, researchers developed the prototypes of the Ethernet, the graphical user interface, the desktop paradigm, the modern personal computer, and its mouse. When these innovations were presented to the senior leadership at Xerox, they could not perceive their potential. The leadership view was, "We are a document company. We have no business playing with these toys." The PARC team was way into the H3 future, and the picture they painted was so fantastically out in the future that senior leaders who were locked in the H1 view could not see it. What was missing? There was no Horizon Two bridging strategy and application. The absence of an effective H2 application at Xerox left the space for Steve Jobs and then Bill Gates. The rest is history.

Years later Steve Jobs would say, "If Xerox had known what it had, and taken advantage of its real opportunities, it could have been as big as I.B.M., plus Microsoft, plus Xerox combined, and the largest high-tech company in the world."

Strategy, Back From the Future

Where do we start the process of creating our desired future?

To begin, we envision our Horizon Three future. With this in mind, we define and develop our H2 strategic initiatives to help us actualize our H3 picture of the future. We then address our H1 imperatives to build credibility and fuel our progress.

How do we create the future?

**To create the future, work from
the future state backward**

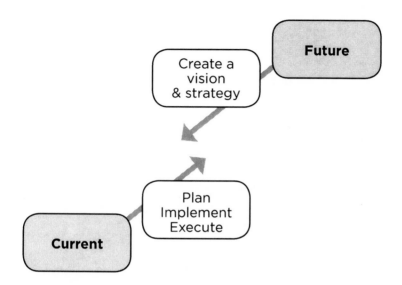

You cannot plan your flight unless you know your destination. Similarly, you cannot plan the development of a new organization before you create a shared picture of the future with the leadership team. To build the organization, we begin by imagining the future we seek to create, then work backwards from there.

Strategic planning is a self-contradicting term. Strategy is a "back from the future" process; planning is the step-by-step process that takes us from here to there. Although we need both processes, planning begins only after we've developed a shared alignment with the overarching themes of our vision and strategy. We must be agile and iterative in our implementation.

How far out your Horizon Three goes depends on your context. Biotechnology and pharmaceutical companies must think ten years into the future. Other companies look three, five, or seven years into the future. For companies delivering software as a service, H3 might be a lot closer.

The Three Horizons

Horizon One 12 months	Horizon Two Two-three years	Horizon Three Three years +
Prescriptive	Adaptive	Explorative
Annual objectives	24 months priorities	Aspirational future
Incremental improvement (Quick wins)	Differentiation (Step change improvements)	Alternative scenarios
↑	↑	↑
Annual objectives	Pilots & initiatives	Transformative vision

Horizon Three conversations are explorative. We envision and articulate transformative visions for our aspirational futures. I use the plural term *futures* because, depending on your context, you may be able to examine a range of Horizon Three pictures of the future.

Horizon Three conversations resist premature convergence. Convergence comes later, when we prioritize our core Horizon Two strategies. Indeed, as the Xerox story reveals, a practical H2 translation designed to bring to life and actualize the H3 vision is the difference between glory and oblivion.

Horizon Two strategies are adaptive. Core strategies are those that a) are essential for success, b) support multiple pictures of the future, and c) enable as many critical elements in these futures as possible. Adaptive strategies must offer clear directional guidance that is relevant through changing environments. We will discuss examples of H2 strategies in the next portal.

First, we begin by imagining the future. To explore H3, we ask:

- Who will we serve?
- What value will we provide?
- What improvements will we deliver?
- What will we be able to do, solve, and contribute three years into the future?
- What are our boldest aspirations?
- What will success look like?

After exploring the future, we work backwards to formulate the strategy and the H2 and H1 priorities:

- Where will we deliver our services?
- How will our solutions and services meet and/or exceed customer expectations?
- How will we differentiate ourselves? What will make our service distinctive?
- Why should others choose to partner with us?
- What will we prioritize?
- How will we create our wins? What will they be?
- What capabilities and systems must we develop to enable our solutions and services?

Insights:

- Horizon Two strategies formulate the critical themes and priorities that enable the transition and evolution from the current state (Horizon One) to the desired future (Horizon Three).

- Core H2 strategies are adaptive, essential for success, and facilitate multiple H3 scenarios.

Process Choreography and the Alchemy of a Strategy Workshop

I explain our approach to the team.

"On its own, an organization has no meaning or strategy. Its meaning and strategy are created by its people.

"How do people create meaning and strategy? Through conversation. An organization is the sum of the conversations among its people.

"Miracles exist. They occur when everyone in the organization shares a picture of the future they believe in, and converses from that future picture."

To create miracles, we must develop a shared picture of the future. We need to answer the vision and strategy questions in ways that include the people around the table, and that allow them not just to see the future, but to see themselves in that picture. That is how we get the propulsion that generates our takeoff velocity.

How do we facilitate the development of an integrated vision that is inclusive of the people around the table?

To achieve breakthrough outcomes, releasing the creative potential of the team is essential. This is both an art and a science. To enable a unified vision to emerge, our process choreography evokes a participative engagement and intensity rather than follows a linear path.

How do we release the creative potential that can produce breakthroughs and dramatically accelerate the process?

Nothing unleashes as much energy, enthusiasm, and creativity as asking people to co-create and imagine their own future. We generate an alternating current by dancing from the foreground to the background and returning to the foreground, and then into the background again.

This work is not merely an exercise in creating nice slides or fancy vision statements. It is about engendering the process that enables people to create the future in their own heads as they converse about it. To realize an audacious, multidimensional future, we must bring together our strategic business priorities (foreground) and the leadership and organizational capacities (background) necessary to produce these outcomes.

The foreground focus includes key business questions we must address:

- What matters most to our clients? How will we meet or exceed their expectations?
- What services and solutions will we deliver?
- What quality will we guarantee? How will we do it?
- How will we produce the expected efficiencies?
- What is our time line for these results?
- What measures will we identify and track to monitor our progress?

The above questions generate foreground conversations. To achieve these results, we unleash the power of the organization, namely its people. This process begins with the leadership team. To build alignment with critical priorities and business issues, and bring in the human element to engage the team's hopes and aspirations, we alternate from the foreground to the background. These background conversations arise from questions such as:

- How will we work together?
- What operating tenets will guide our collaboration?
- Who will we become as a leadership team?
- What matters most to us as we develop our capabilities and build this future?
- How do we create our best work?
- What will we be known for?
- How will we manage challenges?
- What will energize us in the face of corporate antibodies resisting the change?
- How will we bring out the best in each other?

The alchemy of an accelerated strategy workshop is found within the choreography of this dance, in how we engage in a series of conversations by alternating the foreground and the background.

How are we able to produce three months' output of agreements, alignments, and decisions in just three days during our strategy workshops?

To create a breakthrough experience requires that we engage the whole brain. The choreography that integrates the foreground discussions about strategic priorities and the background conversations about who we are and how we plan to evolve as a leadership team engages different parts of the brain. These alternating themes activate different synapses and promote a brain chemistry that results in tremendously positive energy release, which produces the breakthroughs we seek.

Accelerated innovation and transformative results require such an integrated approach. To define the opportunities of the business we develop strategic clarity (foreground) fueled by a set of values and a culture (background) that enable sustainable success. The cerebral focus is integrated with limbic appreciation as new conversations create new synaptic connections in our brains. To create breakthroughs, these processes and synapses must talk with each other so they can innovate and integrate into a new greater whole.

Two and a half years later, the Lufthansa organization is ahead of schedule. They have exceeded their initial plan. However, their greater, more long-lasting success is the new DNA of working and leading that they have fostered and continue to nurture. The value-based, future-oriented leadership is compelling. Stakeholders who initially presented resistance and voiced objections have become advocates and champions. Moreover, the mental models and behaviors we have continued to foster and practice over a series of workshops during this journey have become part of the toolkit of this robust and resilient leadership team.

Practice application:

- To facilitate creativity and innovation and to dramatically accelerate results, alternate and integrate the foreground (conversations about strategic priorities) and the background (who we are as leaders and how will we foster an organizational culture that releases the brilliance of our people).

Portal 8

The Opportunity Zone

Where we focus on the power of Big Bang learning and discover windows of opportunity.

t is 9:30 a.m. on December 29, 2004 when the phone rings in my office. I am packing for tomorrow's long-awaited vacation on the Caribbean shores of Mexico. I pick up the phone and immediately recognize it is Jewell, the head of training and development for WebEx. She and I had collaborated on a series of programs that I had delivered for the WebEx leadership and sales teams. "What's going on?" I ask. Jewell is insightful and to the point, and she directly addresses the reason for her call.

"Dave (head of worldwide sales and later president of WebEx) and I are concerned that we are at risk of losing some of our best people."

"What has triggered this concern? Why might you be losing your best people?" I ask.

"Our teams have been working very hard and we are afraid some of our leaders, like Ryan and Mitch, are experiencing burn-out and could be getting close to their breaking points."

"Well, that's a real concern, Jewell. The risk of losing the best sales leaders on the planet would worry me, too. What do you want to do about it?"

"Well, Dave and I were thinking you might have an idea and that possibly you could help."

"Yes, sure, thank you. Based on what you are sharing, what your leadership team needs is not something like an expensive weekend in Las Vegas that tends to uplift morale for a day or two. For long-lasting results, I suggest you take a different approach."

"What do you have in mind, Aviv?"

"To help your team develop better, more sustainable and renewable cadences in their personal and professional lives, we could introduce them to the core precepts and principles of personal development."

"What does that mean, Aviv? Is this something you can do with our leaders?"

"Yes, Jewell. The best option would be to introduce your team to the Emerald Keys, which represent the core principles of sustained and renewable development. When would you like to begin?"

"As soon as we can."

"How does the first week of February sound?"

Jewell takes three seconds to look at her calendar, and says, "That would be perfect."

We now had a plan. There was only one problem. There was no Emerald, no Keys, and no program ready to deliver. But I had been inspired by the Bill Gates story of selling an operating system to IBM before he had developed it, and I believed I was in a better position to deliver on my promise than Bill Gates had been to deliver on his. I had dedicated two decades to becoming the best teaching instrument possible for personal development by focusing intensely on exploring developmental and spiritual practices, and had nurtured the concept of creating the Emerald Keys. To move it from the back burner, all I needed was an opportunity to give me a reason to engage in the necessary creative writing work. Running a solo consulting practice means I do the R&D, marketing, sales, delivery and deployment, as well as the invoicing and the banking. My guiding business philosophy is to apply the Bill Gates strategy of having my clients fund my research and development. First I sell a program, then I develop it.

Going upstairs, I say to Sara, "I have good news and bad news."

"Give me the good news first," she replies.

"The good news is that I just sold a new program to WebEx. The bad news is I will not have as much time for swimming as I had planned during our ten days' vacation in Playa Del Carmen and Tulum. Since we need to deliver the program in four weeks, I must begin to develop it immediately."

"Oh, I think you will be just fine," Sara says.

I wrote the Emerald Keys program on the Playa Del Carmen beach. The session with the WebEx leadership team became the most impactful program I had delivered to WebEx up to that point. In the following two years, Jewell arranged for a dozen more Emerald Keys programs for the entire sales team, and I went on to produce the eleven Emerald Keys CD set. Under the leadership of Dave, Ryan and Mitch, the WebEx sales team became the most successful inside-sales operation in the world at that time. As WebEx alumni subsequently spread to other companies in the Bay area and around the world, the seeds planted with the Emerald Keys program continued to grow. Eleven years later, in 2015, Dave and Ryan provided me with an opportunity to update the entire Emerald Keys program for their RingCentral sales leadership team.

My Big Bang Learning Moment

Occasionally someone asks, "How did you get started helping executive teams create breakthrough results by accelerating growth and innovation?" My response, "It all began with my Big Bang learning moment."

The point of the story I am about to share is that any moment, including this one, could be your Big Bang learning moment. Moments that appear funny or casual—and even moments that contain an insult—represent Big Bang potential. Recognizing them requires you to be fully awake and present in your life.

My Big Bang learning moment began on a beautiful spring morning in 1978. I was a 19-year-old kid sitting in the briefing room during a fighter pilot course on an airport base in the south of Israel. Just a few weeks into flying practice, 35 colleagues and I felt very good and confident about ourselves. In fact, we were quite cocky. One month earlier we were part of a much larger group, but half of our friends did not make the cut and were sent back to serve as infantry soldiers. Naturally, we felt we were the lucky ones. We were about to fly multi-million-dollar machines. It was thrilling.

In the midst of our banter, in walked our chief instructor. The room became deadly silent. He was a stern colonel and a good pilot himself. His first words, "Listen up everybody," made it clear an important message was coming.

He proceeded, "Now, I know exactly what you are all feeling. I know what you are thinking. You are feeling pretty good about yourselves, like you are the masters of the sky because you have been flying for a bit. You're thinking that soon you'll be fighter pilots in the Israeli Air Force, making you the masters of the universe.

"Now, get this. Flying is not difficult. Teaching someone to fly is not very difficult, either. In fact, if we had 35 monkeys sitting in your chairs, we could teach them to fly. You may be asking yourselves, 'Then why are we sitting here and not the 35 monkeys?' The answer is that within a narrowly defined window of time and budget, the Israeli Air Force must produce a sufficient number of good pilots. We suspect that monkeys would need a lot more flying hours than you, and probably would crash some of our airplanes before they learned to fly safely. Given our constraints, we think you have a better chance of delivering the necessary critical level of performance more quickly and inexpensively than the monkeys. If you learn to land safely during the next couple of weeks, you will qualify for your first solo flight. If it is successful, you will move on to the next training phase."

Now you may think I was offended or upset that our chief instructor compared us to monkeys. To the contrary; I was thrilled and totally mesmerized. For the first time, someone had connected the dots for me by explaining that learning was more than just acquiring a skill. The chief instructor made it clear that learning means providing a desired level of performance within a narrowly defined window. Unless you can deliver it within the given constraints, your efforts will have been meaningless.

Recognizing the true meaning of learning triggered a Big Bang moment that started me on a new and revealing journey. The game-changing realization was that the economics of learning is defined by a critical performance achieved within a limited and narrow time frame.

On that spring morning in the briefing room, my lifelong inquiry into the economics of learning was born. I began to ask questions, such as, Why do some people learn faster than others? What can we do as managers and mentors to help everyone learn faster? How can we accelerate the process of learning application? What methods and practices can turn ideas into actuality more quickly and effectively?

These are the critical questions you grapple with as you lead and mentor your teams. Nothing ever happens in a void. Opportunity shows up within a narrowly defined window. The essence of organizational life, of growth and of success, is much more than learning and innovating. It is about the speed of learning and the velocity of its application.

Insight:

• Living the charmed life is the result of realizing that every moment carries the potential to become a learning Big Bang, a eureka discovery that could redefine what you do and how you approach your endeavors.

Your Window of Opportunity (WOO)

Earlier I proposed that you embrace the three horizons, applying the mental model of near-term, mid-term, and long-term concurrently in a pragmatic way. Here is how you can implement this approach:

1. Develop your Horizon Three by envisioning a series of plausible and desired futures. These H3 lenses help you determine your priorities in H2 and H1.

2. Build your Horizon Two by selecting a few critical strategy themes and priority initiatives (and pilot programs) to develop your H3 options.

3. Accelerate your Horizon One by addressing immediate business imperatives that lead to near-term results (customer needs, cash flow, and capabilities, etc.) and accelerate H3 and H2 by embracing the opportunities that present themselves.

Insight:

• Opportunities come through open windows. How you respond to them defines your results and where you get to play.

Practice application:

• Consider: what opportunity are you focused on right now? What defines the window of that opportunity?

What is a window of opportunity? How does it define your potential to succeed by leading and shaping outcomes?

Right now you are facing a window of opportunity. Can you identify it? Are you able to respond to it?

We all experience opportunities along our journeys. Some come early in life; others come later. You may experience a series of windows of opportunities (WOOs), while others have one big WOO. What is not obvious is the part you play in shaping your window of opportunity. In many situations there are too many unknown elements to predict where opportunity will come. Thus people who excel in business, the arts, and other entrepreneurial pursuits, get up every day ready to discover a big opportunity window.

How do you build the necessary readiness? What capabilities must you build to respond effectively when a window of opportunity opens up? Answering these questions enables us to recognize and leverage the opportunities that present themselves.

Here is how I stumbled on the opportunity window insight. I was 12 years old when my awareness of the acute significance of "WOO" was triggered. I recognized that my cross-country distance running accomplishments that year had opened an opportunity window for me the following year. Since I knew all the best runners in my age group, it became clear that if I focused and worked hard, I could realize the opportunity to become the Israeli champion for the "age 14" group. My interest in pursuing other endeavors meant that if I missed this window, it was not likely to reappear. This was a one season opportunity window. I decided to take it, and I won. Further, earning a series of championships that year became a seminal experience. I realized that opportunity windows compel you to apply yourself and take action.

Here are some of the opportunities that show up in life that are often time sensitive:

- Learning specific skills
- Meeting or exceeding athletic goals
- Achieving academic success
- Meeting influential teachers
- Building relationships
- Capturing specific time sensitive insights
- Finding investment opportunities
- Making career changes
- Escaping war zones
- Surviving natural disasters
- Leveraging a disruptive and transformative trend
- Breaking into new markets
- Participating in a talent show
- Being present in your children's life at critical times

These examples, and so many more, tend to appear within a limited window of opportunity.

In short, your whole life is your opportunity window.

Consider the first employee groups at Google, Amazon, Facebook, and other rapidly growing companies. Working for these companies during their startup stage was an extremely rare window of opportunity, offering once-in-a-lifetime lucrative prospects.

Like others of his generation, my father's survival as a teenager in Europe during WWII is a story of courageously responding to a series of opportunity windows that enabled his escape. Unlike both his parents and three of his brothers and sisters who were murdered in Auschwitz, he miraculously fled Europe to arrive in Israel as a 19-year-old. The ordeal that led to his escape and the subsequent building of a new life in Israel illustrates how one opportunity window may lead to another. For my father, each escape step presented itself as a distinct opportunity to take the initiative and boldly respond by making his move.

Insights:

- Living is about first seeing the opportunities in front of you, then taking action.

- Adaptive and resilient people are prepared to respond to new opportunity windows at every moment of every day.

Your Once in a Lifetime Opportunity

"When you get home, how about you start coaching me just as you coach executives around the world?" the email said. I was in Tel Aviv for meetings, and my wife Sara and son Edan, a junior in high school, were back home in Seattle, when I received this request from my son. I paused to take it in. He had never asked me for anything quite like this. It was clear he had something in mind when he wrote that email.

Now, I have trained myself to be highly alert and attuned to opportunity windows. I bet, when you reflect on it, you will agree that you, too, are highly attuned to shifts and opportunities in spaces that are important to you, about which you care deeply. At that moment, reading this simple one-line request, I sensed tremendous significance and potential. Even though it was not explicitly stated, I felt Edan was saying to me, "I want to start a new phase in our relationship. I want you to address me as a young person on the path to becoming a responsible adult. Therefore, I want us to foster a new kind of dialogue where I can benefit from your coaching experience." That is the message I internalized.

You cannot bake a cake with half the ingredients. Similarly, the window of opportunity practice is about giving an opportunity whatever it needs and deserves, nothing less. I am not speaking about gushing or shouting from the rooftops, even though you may at times feel like doing that. To give an opportunity a full measure of response implies that you meet it on its terms, diligently bringing to the table all the mission-critical components. If the opportunity is a job that requires a ten-foot ladder, it means showing up with a ten-foot ladder, not six foot, not seven foot, not nine foot. Anything lesser than a ten-foot ladder is useless because it cannot get the job done.

Edan's request felt like a once in a lifetime opportunity. Whether or not he fully realized what he was asking, he deserved the full measure of response. Unexpected and extraordinary developments can take place when a door opens and you choose to walk through it.

Immediately after my return, we started weekly meetings. We organized a special time and space for these conversations, just as I do with my clients. After a while, Edan began inviting a few of his friends to join some of the meetings. Soon I found myself in weekly meetings with a circle of 16-year-olds, engaging in conversations about overcoming setbacks, about meaning, purpose, and love, about money, career, and managing one's emotions and energy, about will, discipline, and much more.

Those were unforgettable and precious evenings.

One of these circle meetings started with a question I posed: "If you could change one thing in this world, what would that be and why?"

After a few moments of silence, Dalton spoke. "The one thing I would change in our world is that I would make sure there was a better understanding between the generations. I would initiate real conversations that actually matter, where we really listen to each other. My grandfather must have so much experience and understanding about life and relationships, and about what is important, and my parents, too, but we never talk about these things. It is such a wasted opportunity. I want to know more from them about how they really think and what they really feel, but we don't have such conversations. Mostly we talk about what I should or shouldn't do."

His voice was breaking a bit and his candid courage stirred something in everyone present. He added, "It doesn't make sense. Every generation starts almost from the same point. Yes, technology is different. But in the really important questions about life, like relationships, love and living, experience is not transferred. We don't learn from each other, so every generation seems to repeat the same mistakes."

We all knew something real had just happened. The atmosphere in the room was tender and electrifying. Dalton was expressing a bigger cry. His request for change could not be answered or pacified. His message deserved to be taken in and reflected upon. He was asking us to imagine how different our world could be if we started having meaningful conversations with our children and grandchildren in which we would inquire, listen and seek to understand each other.

I am writing this book for Dalton, and for all the other Daltons who share a similar experience.

But wait, the story doesn't end there. The window of opportunity (WOO) insight is that your response to a current opportunity shapes and creates next and new opportunities.

Our weekly meetings continued through Edan's high school graduation. When he went to the University of Washington, we established a weekly coaching conversation. Every Friday we met to debrief the week, to reflect on what went well, on what could be learned from the experiences of the week, and to develop goals for the coming week.

During our third Friday meeting I posed the following questions to Edan: "For three weeks you've been on campus, on this new leg of your journey. What is the opportunity window here for you? What do you believe is the most important puzzle you need to figure out right now?"

After we explored this question in depth, Edan said, "I need to discover how I learn best. Figuring that out will help me identify what else I need to discover, and what my next steps are."

Throughout Edan's four years at the UW we revisited these two questions on numerous occasions: "What is this window of opportunity about? What is most critical for you right now?"

The answers evolved as the opportunity window changed. At a later stage Edan's answer became, "At this time, the purpose of my education is to help me open as many options as possible, so that when I am ready, I can choose what I want to do from a position of having multiple options, rather than no options."

Then the startup bug hit. Edan went from attempting to start one company to then applying his learning to starting a second, and a third. From here on, he will tell the story if he chooses to share it.

My point here is twofold. First, every opportunity represents a once-in-a-lifetime choice, because today is never coming back. Second, the way you show up today and respond to opportunities here and now determines the opportunities that will find you tomorrow.

Insight:

• Today will never come back. What are you doing right now to respond to and embrace your opportunities? How are you attracting the next new opportunities today?

What Is the Most Difficult "Thing" in the World?

Consider your own career. To date, how have you responded to opportunities that opened up for you?

How have your actions within their respective windows enabled you to recognize and embrace your next new opportunities?

Consider your life-centering experiences, those moments and events that shaped who you are and your view of the world. Which of these occasions occurred in an unexpected way, simply because you showed up at a certain place and time in response to an instinct or an intuition that this was the place you needed to be at that time?

Consider the chain of events that led you to meet important people in your life—a coach, a mentor, a spouse, someone who opened doors for you. When and how did you know this was an important person for you? How did you invest in and build the relationship?

Often you are not aware of the opportunity window in the moment, but recognize it in retrospect. At times, a window is clearly defined by levers outside of your control; in other situations, you can influence and extend the window.

Because I was born and raised in a kibbutz, my exposure to money and the economic equation was delayed. But their significance was revealed in my Air Force learning Big Bang moment. To make the cut to the next phase of the fighter pilot course, I had to demonstrate a safe takeoff and landing after only a few short weeks and a limited number of flights. Bang! Performance is not evaluated in a vacuum. Performance is measured inside a defined and limited situational window.

The insights I gained from flying evolved my understanding of opportunity windows. I was beginning to learn about the "interception window." Getting into a shooting position requires the pilot to enter a maneuver envelope. The interception window is a moving diagram, continually changing with your and your opponent's movements. In a dogfight, the comparative position, velocity, and maneuvering of two very fast flying machines give rise to a critically precise window of opportunity.

When I work with business leaders, we begin by appreciating their opportunity window. We evaluate the landscape, their own assets and strengths, and their near- and mid-term opportunities, threats and vulnerabilities. We then develop proactive and contingent strategies. Proactive strategies are designed to create new windows of opportunity. Contingent strategies build a ready response to plausible exigencies and threats.

Here is an example of a proactive strategy. Imagine the conversation is about your career path. Facilitating the discovery, I would ask what new capabilities you need to develop in the next two years to be considered a credible candidate for an executive role you desire. That is a proactive inquiry.

If the conversation with your leadership team is about delivering new levels of value contribution to the company, and you determine that to move up the value ladder, you need to shift from "reporting-the-news" to "predicting-the-news," and then to "guiding-choices-that-shape-the-news," you quickly realize that you need to hire data scientists and develop cognitive computing capabilities. This is an example of building readiness and positioning yourself to deliver new future value by implementing a proactive "Horizon Two" organizational strategy.

Here is an example of a contingent strategy. On a family trip to Disney World, you all acknowledge that you have differing areas and levels of interest, and you discuss the reality that the venue will be crowded. Thus it is highly likely that you will lose contact with each other. You agree that if this happens, you will gather at a recognizable spot on the next hour. That is a contingency plan for the here and now.

Similarly, the Business Continuity Plan you and your team develop incorporates a variety of plausible scenarios, such as natural disasters, geopolitical events and currency fluctuations.

To achieve your desired outcomes, what proactive and contingent strategies must you create?

Developing thorough and diligent proactive and contingent strategies is integral to mastering your windows of opportunity. Great actors will tell you that thorough preparation facilitates their freedom, allowing them to be in the moment and spontaneous on the set. All they need to do is to show up and be in character and in-the-zone. The rest flows out of that place. "Being in the zone" is another name for being present within your opportunity window here and now.

This is the idea behind the truism, "If you want something done, ask a busy person." It recognizes that people who are best equipped to find the next window are those who are "in the zone" and attuned to the window they are in right now.

Although this statement will sound like a Zen koan, my point is this: "The future is most likely to appear where the future appears."

An obvious case in point is Silicon Valley. As a place where new technology breakthroughs emerge, it is likely to foster the next new massive advances. Though not a certainty, this scenario is plausible because the aggregated know-how of the "in-the-zone" network of people there can be scaled quickly into immense successes.

Think about Apple. The iPod led to the iPhone. The iPhone enabled the iPad. If Steve Jobs had not created the iPod, whether the iPhone and the iPad would have appeared with such an exceptionally wide market readiness and appeal is questionable.

Try this riddle. What is the most difficult "thing" in the world? By which I mean: what is the most difficult challenge to overcome, the most difficult conundrum to solve, the most difficult achievement to bring about?

Don't take a short cut. Write down your answer before you read on.

When I pose this question to various groups I get different kinds of answers. Below are a few responses that are typical. The most difficult "thing" in the world is to:

- win a Nobel prize.
- win an Olympic gold medal.
- quickly recover from setbacks; to genuinely turn lemons into lemonade.
- become a truly leading authority in your field.
- write a bestseller.
- live regret-free.
- be truly happy.
- maintain balance through the ups and downs of life.
- become truly famous.
- become a U.S. president.
- become an astronaut.

Though reasonable answers, they are narrowly framed and short-sighted. I am seeking a bigger, meta level answer, a formulation that is the foundation for many of these and other answers.

The most difficult thing—the most difficult achievement—to realize is not getting rich. It is not being on stage performing or even winning the Nobel Prize. Although the above achievements require a lot of work, dedication and determination, by themselves they are not the most difficult thing in the world.

The most difficult thing in the world is to get all the right ingredients in the right place at the right time.

It is this convergence that creates an opportunity window that may lead to a Nobel Prize, to fame, and possibly to great financial success. The convergence of the right ingredients, in the right place, at the right time.

The story of life and the story of business are that you often get the right ingredients in the right place, but you are too early or too late. Or you may get to your destination in the right time, only to find out it is not the right place after all.

People frequently show up in the right place and at the right time without the right ingredients to leverage their opportunity.

The most difficult challenge to overcome is to bring all three together. The Beatles were in the right place at the right time, and they brought together the right ingredients to become "The Beatles." Usain Bolt, Michael Phelps and Katie Ledecky each showed up at the right time, in the right place, ready to deliver breakthrough results.

Analyze deeply great successes in any arena—in business, the arts, sports, personal relationships—and you will find the synchronization of these three factors.

Considering the convergence of these three factors—right place, right time, right ingredients—makes it obvious that not all three are always within your control. In fact, there are many circumstances that are out of your control. To bring the right ingredients together requires a constant state of vigilance and awareness.

You master your windows of opportunity by being ready. Then, when they present themselves and luck, serendipity or the universe decide to smile upon you, you have the right stuff at the right place in the right time.

Practice application:

Consider and and reflect on:

• What opportunity windows are you responding to at this time?

• What new opportunities do you foresee and expect to shape?

• What capabilities and additional ingredients do you need to bring together to engender readiness?

The Transformation Agent

In which we learn about the drivers for change, the process of adult learning and how to transform broken conversations to address unmet needs.

A four-year-old: "Mother, I love you like the whole world."
Mother: "I love you like all the stars."
Four-year-old: "But mother, if we start competing in love, love will run away..."

The Wow Multiplier

In all the years of my consulting career, I have made only one cold call. In early 2002, Sara and I decided to target Emeritus Assisted Living as a client. I urgently wanted to work with large corporate clients, and we believed the right ingredients were in place to do so. Emeritus was the second largest assisted living company in the U.S., and its headquarters was in Seattle where we live. Sara was an experienced bereavement counselor and as she and I talked one evening, we felt that I had unique value to bring to the table.

I found the corporate headquarters phone number and

called. When a receptionist answered, I asked to speak to the person in charge of training. It would take me five more years to realize that HR and training departments are my least productive entry points into a company, but luckily I did not know that yet. Adora took the call and told me she could see me for 30 minutes the following Tuesday. Years later, she admitted this had been the only time in her career that she had agreed to a cold call meeting.

Walking into Adora's office, I hoped serendipity would be on my side. It was prime time to deliver on my promise to my wife. Twenty-one years earlier, at the age of 22, I had made a radical decision to take the path less travelled. I reasoned that instead of taking the traditional routes in search of success, money, advancement, recognition, and power, only to wake up in my mid-50s and begin asking questions regarding purpose and meaning, I would reverse that order. First, I would pursue the big questions of living, development, purpose, meaning, spirituality, and the higher human potential. At a later stage, I believed the material question would take care of itself, and flow out of the fruits of my journey. Early in life there is a daring conviction that comes with not knowing what you do not know. It is only in retrospect that we learn to appreciate the significance of the convictions that had guided us.

At 42, after two decades of persistent inquiry into the human potential, turning my experience into a commercial success became a pressing need. To enable our family to do what we had hoped, I told Sara I would find a way to achieve a 25-year financial plan in ten years. We both felt that Emeritus Corporation was a natural springboard to the large corporate clients that seek the solutions I was ready to offer.

Though she only had 30 minutes, Adora talked with me for nearly 90 minutes. Rather than join her scheduled meeting, she followed her instinct and stayed in the conversation. "You have to meet my boss, Susan," was Adora's closing comment. The following week I returned to meet Susan. She was intrigued when I proposed to make Emeritus facilities across the country special and different by creating a program to energize their executive directors with a new set of ideas, mindsets, and capabilities that would inspire their work and help them sustain themselves. "I want you to meet my Signature team," Susan said as she called Adora and two other women into the conference room. Susan did not waste a moment. In her spirited way, she went directly to the point. "This is Aviv. He proposes to create a special program for our executive directors. What do you think about this idea?" she asked.

"Well, what will you do with our executive directors?" the three of them asked, looking at me. "Can you give us a preview of your program?"

Although I had spent the previous 15 years conducting development workshops with groups in Israel and the U.S., I still was very inexperienced in corporate settings. It would take me a couple of years to establish the rule that I don't do auditions, but on that day (lucky for me), I went with the flow. Instinctively I knew this was one of those opportunity window moments. "Can I pull off a 'wow' experience?" I asked myself. "Can I access and activate the 'wow multiplier'?"

The wow multiplier insight began to germinate in me at the age of 12 when I observed my mother at work. She had opened the first agency in Israel to represent top classical musicians; she was the first Israeli member of the International Society for the Performing Arts, and later became part of its management team. When I was nine and ten, she took me backstage to meet internationally acclaimed artists such as Jean-Pierre Rampal, Isaac Stern, Daniel Barenboim and Pinchas Zukerman. I learned that a few great virtuosos commanded a disproportionally huge space and percentage of the financial rewards, while other contenders continued to struggle immensely or gave up the dream of a solo career in favor of winning a seat in an orchestra. The winner-takes-all dynamic that would be dramatically accentuated 30 years later by the Internet already was paramount in the music world.

For years I thought about this phenomenon. What was it that made a few so lucky and left everyone else struggling? What were the mechanics of this winner-takes-all dynamic?

Where else did it play out?

I translated this early observation into action to help me launch our business successfully, first in the leadership and talent development market, and then in the strategy and innovation arenas. I framed the wow multiplier phenomenon as the following tenet: "If you do good work, people will see you as okay. If you do excellent work, you will be rated as good. Only outstanding work will be appreciated as excellent. Therefore, the only way to produce an absolutely outstanding memorable effect is to create and deliver a wow impact. If you do wow work, you will be rewarded disproportionally."

This became my brief and operating philosophy: *good is okay, excellent is good, outstanding is excellent. To become memorable, create a wow experience.*

But how could I create a wow impact in an improvised 15-minute workshop simulation?

There was no way to do it in such a short time. Instead, I asked the executives to spend a few silent moments thinking about how to complete the following sentence: "My passionate purpose in life is..." The room grew silent while they each worked to formulate their individual purposes; subtly and quickly, the feeling and atmosphere in the room were shifting. In a couple of minutes, we were transported from the atmosphere of a busy office in downtown Seattle to one similar to the clear, vibrant, and serene atmospheres experienced on mountaintops.

Then the dialogue began. I asked the executives to share what they had written. Then I asked further what these words meant to them, and how they expressed these ideas in their work. I finally was relaxing for the first time since the meeting had begun. The deeper the conversation, the more relaxed I become. The sharing became ever more tender, stimulating, and insight-rich. We were at the deep end of the pool within minutes.

"How do you fulfill your intense corporate responsibilities, work from within the sweet spot of your core competence, and at the same time discover the deeper meaning of your life's purpose? What does it mean for you to be a servant leader?

What practices do you develop to bring these ideas to life? How do you replenish yourself physically, mentally, emotionally and spiritually?"

There was an instant sense of safety, trust, and possibility. "People don't remember what you say, they remember how you made them feel." These four executives who were responsible for the quality of service in hundreds of assisted living communities all around the U.S. genuinely and deeply wanted to impact the elderly who were living in their communities by providing them with the most dignified experience possible. But it was not easy to accomplish these outcomes while also managing the pressures of running an efficient operation that generates profits for the company and returns for its shareholders. Their work was neither conflict free nor friction free. All this was bubbling up in those few minutes, and the executives decided that before deploying a program for their directors, they wanted to experience it with their leadership team. Having sold my first corporate program, I officially was in business. Our mini-workshop created the desired wow impact. My work with Susan continued for five years with a series of leadership seminars, executive coaching and a think tank project on the future of the assisted living industry.

The Triangle of Change

Ron had just landed in the executive chair, the role he had envisioned for himself. Now he must leverage his window of opportunity. Where to begin?

Knowing he had to take action immediately, Ron reached out to me. The challenge he faced was how to make critical changes by rallying his new team and actualizing a new vision and possibility.

"I want to create change. My team must develop a new way of leading and working together if we are to move higher up the value chain," was how Ron started our conversation.

In his new role, Ron was responsible for more than 12,000

employees in a fast moving global organization. He had come to the position with strong leadership convictions and a vision for the business. Most importantly, Ron understood that momentum was critical. To drive change by maximizing his window of opportunity, time was of the essence.

Our conversation immediately moved to a practical focus. Based on his experience, Ron felt that the best way to create results was to unleash innovative solutions with his team by building a highly collaborative environment and resolving execution challenges on the move.

His request was simple: "I know what I want to build and where we need to get to in terms of business results and operational excellence. The question I am wrestling with is, what is the best way to mobilize change quickly and build sustained progress?"

"What is the most natural place for you to kick-start this process? Where do you believe you want to begin?" I asked.

"The simplest and most natural way to begin is to build agreement and a sense of shared mission with my direct team. If we imagine the same destination and agree on our priorities, the rest will flow from our shared picture of the future."

Ron had developed a clear leadership philosophy, and he wanted to find the best and most effective way to transform his vision into reality.

"Yes, this makes complete sense," I agreed. "The next questions to consider are, How will you help your team embrace a new way of working? What are the critical elements of this change process?"

Ron looked at me, smiling. "That's why we are speaking! I expect you to help me accelerate this journey."

"To help your team embrace new ways of working effectively and successfully, you must bring together three elements critical to initiating change. Building the momentum essential to actualizing your vision requires you to integrate a fourth element."

Sketching on the pad in front of me, I drew the Triangle of Change:

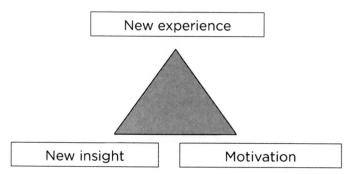

"To create change, the team first must gain *new insight* about the future you seek to enable. This new insight helps raise the awareness necessary to envision and initiate new future possibilities.

"To jump-start the process of building your vision of a high impact entrepreneurial organization, you must cultivate new insights and awareness with your team, ensuring that they understand why the vision is so important, and how it will impact organizational results. No new insight and perception equals no urgent need for change. To build radical trust in the direction you are setting, team members must appreciate and understand the picture of the future you create with them. The new insight is the entry portal to the change process.

"Compelling motivation is the second critical element to create and mobilize change. With new awareness planted within your team, you allow them to discover their individual and collective *motivation*. Motivation is an intrinsic property that people discover by answering the WHY question. The "why" establishes what is in it for each individual—the WIIFM (What's in it for me), and what's in it for the whole team—the WIIFU (What's in it for us). You must unleash the "me" and the "us" motivations.

"However, insight and motivation by themselves are not sufficient to initiate change. If they were, we would see many more people making changes with greater ease. To embrace change we must experience it, and thereby unleash the can-do potential it brings. Therefore, once you have cultivated new insights and motivation, bringing the change to life requires a *new experience*.

"How do we create a new and memorable experience that activates the change you imagine? By bringing the future into the present, allowing people to taste it and experience it. To fully embrace change, we must experience a new way of working. New experience is the portal to change."

"That's exactly my experience, too," Ron responded, looking at me intently. "That's precisely what we need to do. What kind of experience do you have in mind?"

"As you indicated, the way to begin is to create a new shared experience for and with your team. For example, to dramatically accelerate the prototyping of solutions, we must build an agile innovation culture by practicing faster learning loops that are open and transparent. We can simulate these behaviors with your team. By designing a workshop process that facilitates these critical behaviors for the desired future, they can catch themselves operating at a higher level and thus access the knowledge of this modus operandi."

Peak experiences are an essential element in creating and leading change. They become lodged deeply in us because they are different from our routine.

How do peak experiences impact us? They imprint us with new mental models, download new "operating systems," and galvanize fresh ways of working that we then seek to emulate and recreate. Peak experiencers build muscle memories that enable us to reproduce relevant behaviors. For instance, converting ideas into implementable solutions faster requires a new "operating system," by which I mean a new way of working. This is a behavior and muscle memory we bring to life through or in a new experience the team co-creates.

Here's why all three elements of the Triangle of Change are critical:

• **Insight:** Without perceiving the possibilities and the urgent need for change—how tomorrow can be different, and how you can be different in it—you are not likely to initiate the process of change.

- **Motivation:** Without the impetus and passionate desire to lead change and to create new and better conditions for yourself and your team, there will be no forward propulsion or movement.
- **New experience:** Without the new experience that brings the change to life, the proposed future remains abstract, devoid of shared involvement and understanding. Its energy can be released only through action.

Ron gathered his thoughts. "So a new experience is the third element in your change model. What is the fourth component you hinted at?"

"Every aspect of the *environment* is either helping you or holding you back. To accelerate change on the path to a new future, motivation and new experience must be sustained by a supportive and purposeful environment. The physical space, the organizational design, the governance processes and protocols, and the reward and incentives structure all are layers of the environment that either support or interfere with your progress. The environment can hold your team back with the gravitational pull of the past, or propel the team forward by the gravitational pull of the future you are creating together."

Organizational effectiveness is brought about by an alignment that invests all of the team's "organizational calories" purposefully to progress toward creating the desired future state.

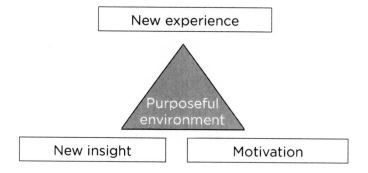

Ron smiled as I completed this quick sketch on the pad. It seemed to validate his own experience. "You are absolutely right. In my experience, to initiate and sustain change, we need this fourth element, which actually is comprised of many components that make up the environment. Though not every aspect is in our control, the control points we do own must align with our purpose."

Thinking for a moment he added, "I have seen that this is true within all aspects of life. To create change in my lifestyle, health, relationships, and certainly in our work as a team, we must create these three elements first, and then invest in building a supportive and purposeful environment that will help us realize our vision."

Good models do just that—they validate what people already know based on their experience, even though it never has been made explicit. A useful mental model simplifies and accelerates the translation of ideas into action.

Three weeks later, Ron and I met with his leadership team to embark on the journey of co-creating a new future. Together we envisioned the opportunities ahead. During the first day, the team agreed to resist the urge to bring up obstacles that would limit their capacity to imagine their Horizon Three" future.

We followed a simple brief to never begin a change effort by focusing on potential obstacles and limitations. They provide an alibi for the status quo, theologize no action, and cement a "doom loop." Using limitation as your anchor prevents you from engaging the "virtuous loop" of growth opportunities— the engine that mobilizes change and enables you to realize new audacious aspirations.

The dynamic change Ron had envisioned got underway. His team created a new peak experience. They developed a sense of shared ownership and were motivated by their inspiring vision. The natural next step was to mobilize the organization to build the Horizon Two chosen priorities.

Insights:

- Creating accelerated and sustainable change requires insight, motivation, new shared experience, and a purposeful environment that enables and encourages the future state.

- Without the impetus and passionate desire to lead change and to create new and better conditions for yourself and your team, there will be no forward propulsion.

- In the absence of an experience that downloads a new "behavioral operating system," there can be no access to a new future.

Why do I believe so strongly that change is possible, despite challenges, when we bring these four elements together?

I have witnessed and facilitated this transformational change process with hundreds of teams. I have seen skeptics and cynics release themselves from the doom loop and take positive action. I have observed the gravitational pull of yesterday giving way to the forward pull of an inspiring tomorrow. I also have experienced the enthusiasm, energy, and almost miraculous can-do power and action that are unleashed as teams are pulled forward by a shared vision of the future. This acceleration and energy release are tremendously satisfying and inspiring for everyone involved.

Practice application:

- How must your organization evolve to enable and meet the future you hope to realize? What changes must you instigate?

- Outline the insight: What perspectives are critical to catalyze urgency and facilitate movement? How will you frame these insights to be most relevant?

- Cultivate the motivation: Ask your team members what these changes represent for them and for the team. What excites them about the future?

- Facilitate a new experience: Design a special initiative with your team. How will you work differently? How will you collaborate and create results in a whole new way?

- Build a purposeful environment: What kind of support is needed? How will you design the environment, your governance, processes and protocols to help pull your organization forward toward the future you imagine?

The Descartes Trap and the Four Stages of Adult Learning and Transformation

The Descartes trap is a classic mistake leaders make. Descartes' famous words were *cogito ergo sum*, which is Latin for "I think, therefore I am." The Descartes leadership trap is the belief that "I think, therefore it is," and "I think, therefore we are."

Expressions of the Descartes trap are evident when a leader assumes that because a thought or concept is clear in his head, it surely is clear to the rest of the organization. Of course this is sheer lunacy—it amounts to believing that the organization is attuned and aligned by some psychic and clairvoyant powers. While people often are highly sensitized to the psychological drama of their leaders, this provides another strong reason to build effective communication channels and strategy, and to ensure that teams are engaged in co-creating the organizational destiny.

There is another problem with Descartes' assertion—thinking by itself will not get you very far. Philosophy majors will quarrel with me about this issue, claiming I am missing the point of Descartes' proclamation, which was that simply the act of doubting one's own existence serves as proof of the reality of one's own mind and thereby of the self as a thinking entity. At the very least, I would update Descartes' statement as follows: "I learn, therefore I am." In a rapidly shape-shifting environment, if you are not learning, you already are dead.

How do leaders escape the "I think, therefore we all are on the same page" Descartes trap?

They lead from the inside. They are curious and attuned to their own evolving learning. They connect with their teams through a variety of channels. They assimilate diverse points of view. They work to be the facilitators and agents of transformation and growth. They engage in conversations with all stakeholders.

As in Ron's case, executives typically call me when their goals include making a major impact on their business by effecting transformational change. Our collaboration requires us to sidestep the Descartes trap, and render the implicit explicit by engaging their team in co-creating the future.

In a competitive environment, a senior leader's job is to ensure that his teams have the capacity to address challenges proactively so they may take advantage of opportunities posed by a world in which disruptive technologies, new business models, economic pressures, and shifting customer demands are the norm.

Insight:

• In a rapidly shape-shifting environment, your ability to learn ("learn-ability") is your most critical competence.

Consider your own team. How must your organization transform in the next 18 months to meet the opportunities that present themselves? How will you help your team co-lead the transformation effort?

Ron and his team had an urgent mandate to transform the organization. It was clear that meeting this need required work at the strategic, the organizational, and the personal levels. To build the capabilities necessary to implement and lead the change, we had to help the leadership team integrate their own personal growth inside the organizational evolution.

To enable leadership teams to jump-start an accelerated transformation that compresses months of work into just a few days, we must address the whole system—the business, the organization and the leaders, both as a team and as individuals.

Once again we begin by asking the team to take ownership of the future they imagine. We then design a series of conversations to help people engage their learning muscles. We build the excitement needed to create and sustain forward momentum.

These are audacious goals. Facilitating a shift from merely *learning* new information to *internalizing, applying,* and *teaching* it to others requires focus and effort. We must lean on people's self-interest and capacity for personal growth.

To truly effect personal growth and transformational change, we must rely on the four stages of adult learning. Here are the stages we incorporate in our process design:

- Stage 1   Receive

- Stage 2   Understand

- Stage 3   Apply

- Stage 4   Teach/own

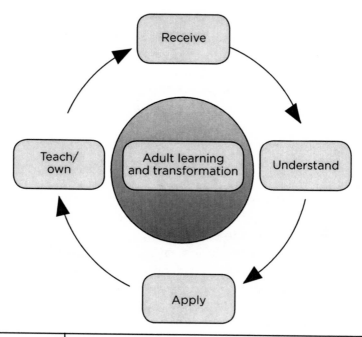

Stage 1	*Receive* I take in new information
Stage 2	*Understand* I internalize the information and validate its implications.
Stage 3	*Apply* I "run water through the pipes" to use the learning in specific situations.
Stage 4	*Teach/own* I model the new learning for others, thus taking responsibility for the continuation of the learning cycle.

Here is how I applied the four learning stages insight at a recent leadership summit with 120 managers that I facilitated for an organization going through rapid evolution. To help the managers accelerate their personal and collective learning, we created a series of experiences that quickly guided participants through the four stages of adult learning and transformational change.

First, we introduced new information about the future of the organization and identified the behaviors and mindsets critical for success.

Second, we enabled the 120 managers to internalize and validate the new organizational information by discussing the implications for each one of them in groups of three.

Third, to address a series of real life problem-solving situations, we had participants engage in breakout groups. These experiences helped participants see the relevance of the information, and enabled them to move from internalizing the learning to applying it.

Fourth, we activated the stage of co-creating, teaching and co-owning the desired outcomes by developing their solutions to these challenges and presenting their recommendations to senior leadership.

The summit enabled managers to test their new knowledge and skills. Practicing and coaching each other in new behaviors made the experience fun and energizing. By the time they returned to the office, the managers had applied a new set of behaviors; they felt they owned the new strategies and were ready to teach their teams what they had learned.

This example illustrates a broad scale organizational process of learning and growth. It is enabled by conversation, which is the currency of organizational life.

Insight:

- When people are given an opportunity to shape their own destiny and future, what becomes possible is nothing less than miraculous.

Working with leadership teams in this way to design innovation and transformation efforts can save six months of precious time as well as tons of organizational calories. By recognizing their window of opportunity and guiding the organization through prototyping solutions for real business issues, leaders develop new capabilities and build commitment to, and ownership of, the desired change.

The personal discovery and growth they experience are what make this type of learning process thrillingly rewarding for managers.

Practice application:

• Design your workshop process to help your teams receive, understand, apply and take ownership of the change you envision.

Converting Complaints into Proposals: A Samoan Circle in Shanghai

It is the last day of a workshop in Shanghai with 80 Hewlett-Packard managers from China, India, Malaysia, and Mexico. We have been working to integrate four groups into one unified global team with a shared mission and joint delivery framework. There are cultural differences and competing agendas. Each of the four centers hopes to grow. At the same time, there is one unified charter: to deliver consistent and optimized service.

We are heading for our lunch break when Eric, the executive leading the newly formed organization, says to me contemplatively, "Thanks to you, we've developed our priorities, integrated a shared language and new frameworks that quickly enabled us to trust one another so we can build our collaboration. Could you guide us into the next step? If there is a way to help us bring our agreements to life and practice our chosen behaviors in the last three hours after lunch, it would provide us with great value."

The request from Eric is intuitive. He is searching for a safe pathway to help his team experience their chosen values in action, and exercise the behaviors they had agreed to demonstrate. I thrive on such moments of challenge. Eric provides me with an opportunity to walk my talk and practice the workshop design principles that I had introduced on the first day:

1. Play improvisational jazz, not a fixed musical score.
2. Allow for divergent and convergent discussion cycles.
3. Alternate the foreground (what) and the background (how).
4. Build on our individual and collective strengths.
5. Unleash the collective knowledge and wisdom of the team.

Eric is asking me to play jazz, and have his leadership team join in and harmonize the melody. After a quick lunch, I get back to our meeting room to collect my thoughts. I set up a Samoan Circle of five chairs in the middle of the room. To fashion a conversation scenario that builds safety, I must set the right tone. I am about to ask people to take a step forward and raise the level of transparency and disclosure by framing specific requests and concerns.

We are about to engage in a new experience, to explore an open and emergent conversation, where there is a great degree of unknown. Once you open the door and invite people in, you have to go with the flow. I cannot be certain that this activity will work; still, I feel a sense of serenity and confidence.

Designing a peak experience requires a combination of know-how, technique, intuition, and core conviction about why you do the work that you do and an unadulterated belief in the process. It further demands a strong belief in the goodness of people and their desire to succeed in improving their conditions.

Although mastery is important, there is something even more critical than ultimate proficiency. People respond to how you make them feel about themselves. Your ability to make people feel good about themselves is determined by the reasons that motivate and guide your work. I bring to the table an unabashed conviction about people's ability to create breakthroughs. Why? I have seen it happen time and time again.

I know for a fact that we all are capable of stepping up, and that every person I meet is uniquely creative, smart, and generous at core. If I am able to facilitate the environment and guide a process to bring forward the best in the managers I work with, then in 99 percent of situations they will surprise each other and themselves with their capacity and what they are able to create. Executives have told me on numerous occasions, "In three days, your process has enabled us to produce three months' worth of agreements and shared decisions."

My conviction and unapologetic expectations that we all suspend disbelief engenders a field of possibility. This space of possibility is what I strive to create as I fashion the ecology that will enable people to speak their minds, transform, and emerge anew.

How do we configure a conversation that will bring to life new ways of working together, and help managers land in a place of agreement, ready for fast deployment?

Though easy to frame, the pivot we use to convert concerns into requests is difficult to apply.

Insight:

- A complaint is the misdirected energy of an unaddressed or unmet need.

Unless a complaint is traced to its root cause and resolved, it tends to produce ineffective and displaced conversations and not address the true concern.

Displaced Conversations

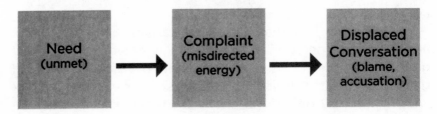

Far too many dialogues are displaced from the instigating need. Such dialogues camouflage the trigger point of concern by dealing with distracting secondary issues. The energy of the concern, and the unaddressed and unmet need, then is misdirected and becomes confused. It appears as a complaint, which triggers a complaint-based interaction that centers on secondary side effects. Displaced interactions cannot resolve the instigating need.

In our process, we seek to name the unnamed, render the implicit explicit, and remedy the displacement by connecting the conversation to the point of origin. The process encourages participants to articulate proposals that help address the need.

Efficacious Conversations

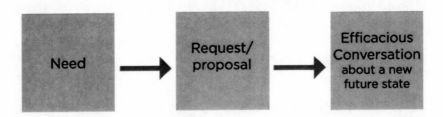

After the team returns from lunch, I explain the roving nature of the Samoan Circle experience. Our focus is on enabling and empowering the voices that want to come forward. This is about making space to speak the unexpressed and to name the unspoken safely. One by one people come forward to discuss their hopes for the global organization. The first few struggle.

I intercept them halfway through their sentences to introduce new language.

"I don't think we can truly be a unified team as long as people protect their space and hold back on information sharing" is an example of an honest complaint. It is framed with a tinge of blame and articulated in closed language that offers no opening for a remedial prospect. How do we express a concern in terms that initiate a productive dialogue?

I propose a reframed language pattern: first articulate the group's common objective. Then explicitly state what need must be met to allow you to enable that outcome. Finally, frame the request.

For most people, stating a need and formulating a request is not easy. It is not a skill we practice early in life, and the managers struggle to internalize this approach. I am asking them to rescript beliefs, positions, and concerns into open and malleable language. We encourage each other with healthy humor. The experience is both raw and liberating. After a few attempts, the manager reframes his initial statement as: "I believe we can improve agility and customer responsiveness. To help us create this outcome, I need to feel confident that we are sharing information openly. My request is that we all demonstrate that we are forthcoming with sufficient details about our projects."

"How does it feel to speak this request?" I ask.

"It feels a little strange, but it actually brings a sense of relief just to say it like this."

One by one people step up to the five chairs in the middle to respond to each other's requests and proposals, and to ask clarifying questions. I coach and facilitate the dance. I intercept backward-looking language and ask people to reframe what they are trying to say into forward-looking language. One manager starts explaining why something cannot work. I ask her to reframe by describing what must be true for the process to work. Thinking this way is a revelation to her.

A third manager inside the Samoan Circle picks up the speaking ball and struggles to formulate what he wants to say.

I ask him to complete these two sentences: "My concern is....
Therefore, the proposal I'd like to make is..."

His first and second attempts focus on other people and
teams. I gently urge him to state the concern explicitly and
then make a concrete proposal to address it. In a moment of
clarity, the new brain circuitry connects and he makes the leap:
"My concern is that we will lose critical elements of our existing
portfolio in our center, and as a result we would lose some of
our core capabilities. I am worried about this negative loop. I
need to know that our interests are looked after, and that as we
build our global team to meet the needs of the business, we
recognize and foster the strengths of our service centers. My
proposal is that we establish a governance cadence that will
provide regular points of review so that we can see holistically
that we are building a sustainable delivery model by remaining
true to our service commitments without penalizing any of our
centers."

The articulation of his concern and the concrete proposal
energizes the conversation, enabling it to take a giant leap
forward. The clear framing invites specific responses that build
meaningfully on his proposal. His comment also makes it easier
for the next series of speakers to articulate their concerns,
needs, and proposals.

Once one person breaks through a blockage, others follow
quickly. As more people demonstrate the new mindset and
language, they are added to the leadership team's behavioral
toolkit, making it easier for them to emulate the behavior of
transforming complaints into proposals.

There is more. This experience helps to make the complicated manageable, and the hard simpler. Discovering the ease
of formulating safe requests makes the seemingly mundane
graceful. For a moment in time, the conditioning that impossibility begets impossibility is neutralized. Our conversation
develops a cathartic healing that brings people together in a
profound way and gives them a reason to believe that they can
shape their destiny.

What creates new futures?

A liberating process that gives people reason to believe they can create their own tomorrows and influence their destiny.

Practice application:

• Begin with the objective the organization is seeking. Explicitly state a need that must be addressed to achieve the objective. Frame the request to achieve the desired behavior or outcome.

An In-Flight Diplomacy Seminar on the Way to Boston

Leading transformational change often requires the wisdom of diplomacy.

A few days after my conversation with Nicholas the astronaut (*Portal Two*), I headed from Seattle to Boston to conduct a leadership workshop. During the flight I sat next to a distinguished diplomat. As the British ambassador to the UN from 1987 to 1990, Sir Crispin Tickell had consulted with heads of state throughout the world. At 78, he was witty and sharp, with tremendous insight and a broad knowledge of current affairs. He remained highly involved in sustainability issues and active on numerous geopolitical and global fronts.

After touching on the big geopolitical questions of the day, I asked the ambassador (you guessed it), "What are the key principles that guide effective diplomacy?"

Developing his answer through anecdotes and stories, Sir Crispin offered the following five principles:

1. Trust
2. Knowledge
3. Mutual interest
4. Engagement
5. Timing

First, the involved parties have to build *trust*. The conversation cannot begin without an initial belief in the other party's good intention. Initial trust eventually builds a deeper trust.

Second, the parties must bring comprehensive *knowledge* of the issues to the table. Knowledge is essential to building credibility, and credibility builds deeper trust. There cannot be a substantive discussion that generates real, practical, and pragmatic solutions without in-depth knowledge.

Third, the parties need to appreciate each other's *interests*. They have to think beyond the concept of win-win, to that of "we" together—a "we" that addresses the interests of those involved.

Fourth, the parties must be in conversation and develop an ongoing *engagement*. The secret to the United Nations Security Council's effectiveness in Sir Crispin's day was that the five permanent Security Council ambassadors held monthly meetings at his apartment. The ongoing engagement developed trust, a comprehensive understanding of the issues, and an appreciation of each other's interests. At crisis points, the reservoir of goodwill caused by their engagement and ongoing conversation became a natural catalyst that enabled joint resolutions.

Finally, *timing* is everything in diplomacy. It is not enough to have the right solution; it must appear at the right time.

On this occasion, I immediately could appreciate the gift Sir Crispin had shared with me. I shared the translation of my in-flight diplomacy seminar with the leadership group the following morning. As leaders and agents of change, our work begins by building trust. It continues by demonstrating knowledge and competence. Appreciating the interests of all people involved leads to the readiness to be fully engaged. We then can create solutions and deliver what is needed and what we are called to do at the right time.

Insight:

- You become an agent of transformation by demonstrating how you lead change, own and apply your learning, convert resistance and complaints into growth opportunities. Building mutual trust and knowledgeable engagement facilitates new shared futures.

Practice application:

- What opportunities are available to you to apply the five principles of effective diplomacy?

  1. Build trust
  2. Cultivate knowledge
  3. Appreciate the top interest of the people involved
  4. Foster positive engagement
  5. Time your conversation and solution

Portal 10

The Wings of Purpose

In which we define mission, vision, and purpose, and discover the power of culture.

E very year Sara and I go on an outdoor retreat to surround ourselves with nature and beauty. In the late 1990s we explored the Oregon shores and hiked to Cape Lookout, a sliver of land extending into the Pacific Ocean. About two thirds of the way, we came upon a very large tree. Sitting down next to it to catch our breath, we realized this large tree was actually growing out of the remnants of the trunk of a much larger tree. Upon careful examination, I concluded the standing tree likely was 120-140 years old. The broken tree from which the new tree had grown must have been even older when it was struck down. The remaining old trunk was huge. Perhaps it was 240 or 350 years old when it was damaged some 120 to 140 years ago. This meant the old broken tree was standing some 400 to 500 years ago.

How powerful was the storm that came through this forest and broke a 250-year-old tree?

Seeing one tree growing out of the other made us think. Nature was offering us a piece of ancient wisdom. Part of the huge root system of the old tree remained intact. Instead of the entire system atrophying when the tree was broken, it was able to redirect its flow to grow a new tree. The resulting beautiful tree utilized part of its predecessor's old root system. The lesson was clear: nature never wastes a "failure." Nature utilizes whatever it can, all the parts, everything.

What Jim the Beachcomber Can Teach All of Us

During my regular morning visits to the semi-private Florida beach near our winter home, I observed a man who cleans the beach daily. He is an odd sight among the fishermen and the surfers.

Morning after morning, I watched him trace the beach with his plastic bag and arm extension pick-up tool. One morning my curiosity got the best of me, and I decided I had to find out the story behind his daily ritual. What compelled him to clean the beach?

Until that morning I had done what we humans tend to do when observing others: we make up stories to explain or justify their actions. The conscious mind does not like incomplete pictures; it is agitated by unresolved riddles. To alleviate the agitation, we complete the pictures and resolve the riddles. We produce our own scripts. We are each the movie producer and director of our imaginative minds. I learned this truth by discovering time and again that I had pre-judged situations incorrectly, and made up a "movie" that was far from reality.

Because I love finding the truth about situations, I've learned to ask others to tell me their story. Here is my revealing conversation with Jim, the angel beachcomber.

"My name is Aviv. If you don't mind my asking, when did you start cleaning this beach? What makes you do it every day?" I began.

Pointing to his heart, Jim said, "I had a heart problem and the doctor told me I should exercise. As I started walking down this beach every day, I quickly noticed it was a landfill. There was too much waste and junk on this beautiful beach to my liking. My immediate reaction was that someone must clean it up. Then I thought, why shouldn't that someone be me? This was three years ago."

"What have you discovered in looking after the beach every morning?" I asked.

"My first discovery was that picking up trash is better exercise than just walking. The second was that a little cleaning every day goes a long way. The third lesson was that I feel good when I leave the beach a little cleaner every day."

"Thank you. I appreciate what you do. Every time I see you, I feel grateful, because this beach is much nicer because of your efforts."

"Well, thank you. I do it first for myself. It's a great exercise and it makes me feel good," replied Jim.

Jim, I realized, was carrying a simple and powerful message: the best way to help yourself is by helping something or someone else. You serve yourself best when you serve a cause. You resolve your needs by addressing the needs of others.

Sooner or later, we discover that responding to the needs of others is a way to address our own needs. In business, you thrive by becoming the answer to your clients' needs.

Insight:

- The receiving is in the giving. By serving a cause you believe in, you serve yourself.

- Paraphrasing President John F. Kennedy: "Ask not what the answer to your question is; ask what question you carry the answer to."

Practice application:

- To what needs are you the solution?

- What will you do today to begin meeting those needs?

The Purpose-inspired Organization

As we have seen, creating the future is much more than articulating a vision or even building a strategy. Creating the future is about bringing to life our vision, mission, strategy, and values through the conversations we create. We build the future through the choices we make and the activities we prioritize and demonstrate.

Having helped thousands of executives embark on the adventurous process of creating a new desired future, I have learned to not impose a rigid process. The context is different in each situation; the landscape varies from one circumstance to another; the opportunities are unique; and the team members' maturation levels, individual aspirations and flexibility vary. Instead, I conduct a series of discovery interviews to learn about the organization and its context. Then I develop a customized approach that best meets the situational needs.

This approach allows me to create the greatest, most sustainable impact in the shortest time possible by building on the strengths of the team and addressing vulnerabilities and blind spots. These executives and companies pay handsomely for my services because our collaboration yields significant value for them. We create this breakthrough collaboration in the way we integrate my approach into their process. I don't ask them to be different. Rather, I encourage them to be new and renewed in themselves by applying the law of the tree (*Portal Five*).

Rick Hughes, the CPO of Procter & Gamble, described my approach this way: "Here is how you are different, Aviv. Most of the large consulting firms come here, interview us, download our brains, go home and convert what they had heard from us into a fancy set of slides, and then come back to tell us what we had told them. Your approach is very different. You helped us unleash our own creative capabilities by integrating your approach into our process. You enabled us to pull it all together and create movement in the organization by designing and facilitating a unique process for us. You deliver a very different outcome than other consultants."

Ted Clark and I collaborated for over six years when he was the Senior Vice President and General Manager leading the Notebook business unit at Hewlett-Packard during its rapid growth years. One day he was asked, "There are many McKinsey and other large consulting firms walking up and down the HP corridors. Why do you work with Aviv? How is Aviv different?"

Ted laughed and said, "With most of these consulting firms the result we get is we end up with fewer people and more work that we need to do, and we become less of a team. With Aviv's help, we visualize where we are going, cultivate the skills necessary to lead the organization from point A to point B, and become more of a team on this journey so we can be successful when we get there. That's why you need Aviv."

Purpose, mission, and vision can be much more than a nice slide or a poster. But by themselves, without the activities, behaviors, and resource allocation choices that bring them to life and animate the organization, they have little meaning and lack the power to inspire breakthrough results and new futures.

We often include a conversation about purpose in the development of the Horizon Three future (*Portal Seven*) of the organization. For some teams, the inquiry about the future is best accessed through the exploration into vision and mission. In each case I adapt and curate these conversations according to the situational opportunities and needs.

In early stage and startup companies, I have advised teams to access and define their purpose by answering the following questions:

- Who do we help?
- How do we make clients better as a result?
- What problems do we solve?
- What is our unique value proposition?

I lead these conversations in both emergent and structured scenarios. People often assume they have answered these questions already. We discover they have not when we slow down the discussion and put a magnifying glass to the inquiry. By following our guidelines to state their answers clearly, and by refining their definitions iteratively, they are surprised to discover how diverse are the points of view around the table.

With other teams, we explore the organizational mission by inquiring about imperatives. I then ask people to answer the following questions:

- What are your business imperatives?
- What imperatives guide the work you do every day?
- What imperatives are forcing change and how must you evolve as a result?

In situations where the team is more attuned to the vision search, I anchor the conversation with the following questions:

- What is your winning aspiration?
- What are your most audacious hopes?
- How do you hope to be able to describe your success three years from now?

Do You Know Yourself?

During a recent flight to Palm Beach, the woman sitting next to Sara told this story about her daughter. After completing seven years of study, first in nursing school and then shifting direction, the daughter finally became a chiropractor. Once she graduated, however, she decided she did not want to practice her profession. Why? She discovered she did not like touching people.

It took seven years to find out that she did not like touching people. This woman's story is not unique. There are many doctors, lawyers and other professionals who spent years studying and perhaps interning, only to discover they do not like their chosen field.

Why does it take some people years to find out that they are directing their effort, time, resources, and dedication to a profession that does not meet their needs, or at the very least, they do not enjoy? Why spend so much time to discover you do not like touching people? Did the daughter study this field to satisfy her mother? Did she become a chiropractor against her own wishes? What caused her to be so distanced from herself?

In this particular situation, we do not know the answers. What we do know is that people can be so distanced and displaced from themselves that they do not know the first thing about what they are like, what their natural inclinations and talents are, what energizes them and what they would enjoy doing.

The journey of life is about finding out what we are like, discovering our talents, and learning about our gifts. The task we face is to be able to fast-forward this discovery process whenever we can, because we can then share more of our gifts in the precious little time we have here on Earth. This is your journey, too. Find out what you love doing, what energizes you, what your purpose is, and then act on it and live your purpose fully.

Do not doubt for a second that you are here for a reason, that your life has a purpose, that you are here to use your gifts to make a difference. I invite you to reflect on these questions:

- Are you where you ought to be?
- Are you learning and growing?
- Do you feel in touch with your true gifts or do you feel distanced from yourself?
- What do you believe you are here to do? How are you meant to make a difference?
- What fills you with energy? When are you most joyous?

Practice application:

1. Make a list of all the things you enjoy.
2. Identify everything you have ever excelled at doing. Think back to the beginning of your career, and even earlier, to your school days. What were you really good at doing?
3. What do you look forward to? What activities do you make a point of not missing?
4. Discover the convergence of items on lists 1, 2 and 3.
5. Actively seek opportunities to express your talents and interests. They may be present inside what you are already doing. Look at what you do in a new way.
6. Give yourself chances to try something new.

What Comes Before MVP

In the National Basketball Association (NBA), "MVP" connotes the Most Valuable Player award presented to the league's best-performing player of the season. In the process of product development, "MVP" stands for the Minimum Viable Product sufficient to validate the concept and the assumptions guiding the development process. Testing the Minimum Viable Product significantly reduces the cost of development, enables developers to bring solutions to market early, and subsequently accelerates new features and versatility.

In the NBA you play to win. In product development you acquire the funding for the next development phase by validating the product concept. In both cases the purpose, mission, and vision (PMV) are clear. Hence, PMV (Purpose, Mission, Vision) comes before MVP.

Here is a simple way to define and offer distinctions among purpose, mission, and vision.

PURPOSE is our reason for being. It describes what we are here for—what we are on this planet to accomplish.

MISSION is how we enact our purpose. It describes how we

express and serve our reason for being.

VISION is the realization of our mission. It describes what the world will look like when we fulfill our purpose by delivering on our mission.

PURPOSE answers:
• Why we do what we do.
• Why we want to get to where we are going.

MISSION answers:
• What we do to get there.
• With whom. How.

VISION answers:
• Where we want to be.
• What it will look like when we get there.
• How the world will be different because of our contributions.

How do we bring purpose, mission, and vision to life?

We translate them into concrete priorities within our strategy. We allocate resources to support these priorities. We ensure that everyone in the organization has a clear line of sight that allows them to see how their work activities embody the purpose, and directly contribute to the mission and the strategy.

As my conversation with Anne (*Portal One*) revealed, we actualize the mission, vision, and strategy when they guide our daily conversations, choices and behaviors.

Give Your Strategy Wings

There is a reason why I alternate the foreground and background in the choreography of our workshops. The saying, "Culture beats strategy" has been around since the 1980s. Management guru Peter Drucker is believed to have said that, "Culture eats strategy for breakfast." In both cases, the message is the same:

a strategy cannot succeed without an organizational culture that supports it.

Choose your preferred metaphor. Strategy without culture is like a bird without wings; it cannot fly. If you prefer the engineer's view, you can say strategy is like a plane without wings; it may accelerate but it cannot take off because without wings there is no lift. Simply put, you cannot develop an effective strategy without the implicit culture required to execute it. Culture provides strategy with its lift.

An organization's future is defined by the integration of vision, strategy, and culture rather than by a point on the map that marks its location or defines a destination. Creating the future is as much about how we show up in our desired scenario as it is about the outcomes and benefits that the envisioned future allows.

How do we create new futures?

We are forever entering and creating new portals of possibility. We are constantly moving into the new tomorrows we attract. The mental model that I propose is that you embrace this day as the conversation that can open new spheres of possibility tomorrow. Contrast this paradigm with the prevailing model in which people think of today as merely the summation of all their yesterdays. When I help teams create their future, my objective and interest are to bring holistic architecture thinking to our process.

Consider creating a compound set of outcomes by integrating multiple inputs. Think of a specific situation that requires you to consider half a dozen interrelated inputs that together produce a number of critical outcomes. Integrating strategy with culture into an experience architecture that brings the culture and strategy to life is one such example.

What are the design principles that guide our experience architecture?

First, we alternate the foreground (strategy) with the background (culture) to create an experience that integrates the two, accelerates learning and discovery, and creates the three buckets of value I describe in the next portal.

Second, we alternate "structure-precedes-content" with "content-guides-structure" to facilitate the flexible integration of both format and emergent conversations. We take a jazz-playing approach, allowing both modalities to alternate and integrate.

There are phases in every project that benefit from a clear structure within which to evolve the outcomes we seek. Then there are moments when the structure must recede into the background to let the emergent content and ideas lead. These are the times that require us to let go of the fixed agenda and timetable and follow the energy of the conversation wherever it leads us.

How do we enable new emergent futures?

By nature, the creative process that enables new futures is extemporaneous. Our job is to go with the flow of this extemporaneous element, much as a surfer rides a wave, or as the improv artist follows the ad-lib discovery of the dialogue.

How do I translate this approach into workshop choreography?

I ensure the team experiences what we explore. Our interactions are designed not just to talk about the culture, but rather to practice and experience the behaviors we intend to create inside the context of the strategy. This is what we achieved in the Samoan Circle in Shanghai with the group of HP managers (*Portal Nine*), and applying the three horizon approach with the Lufthansa leadership team (*Portal Seven*). In each situation, I seek to transform how we get work done by facilitating and engendering shared experiences that integrate the culture component with the strategy. The shared experience creates a muscle memory the team subsequently is able to access on their own when they go back at work.

The awareness that people embrace new behaviors when they experience positive and rewarding results guides the design of the first three hours of every workshop. My goal is for everyone in the room to experience their first breakthrough before we go to lunch. This is a workshop design objective: facilitate a series of interactions that promote personal realizations and collective "ahas" before lunch on day one.

I am asking the busy managers who attend my workshops to step into a zone of intensified engagement and refrain from multi-tasking for three days. In return, I promise them an experience with a significant return-on-engagement (ROE), a return-on-focus (ROF), and a return-on-intensity (ROI). By applying and practicing this approach, we generate a dramatic return-on-time (ROT), and specifically a dramatic return on their conversation time. These managers experience the excitement of their creative collaboration and discover the velocity of results they generate in an open, transparent, and trusting environment.

Open collaboration does not happen "out there." We want to experience its benefits right here, right now. We want to feel the power of converting complaints into requests and proposals, and to discover the mindset shift from inputs and activities to outcomes and value. By learning and modeling these behaviors, the team spontaneously builds the capacity to replicate and flex these muscles as needed. Capabilities and skills developed inside the team's work are five hundred times more impactful and sustainable than those introduced in a sterile learning environment separated from the work. A memorable and replicable working experience creates great business value.

Such experiences cause people to say, "This workshop created the value of three months' work in just three days. Not only did we develop our vision and strategy, we also created a deep sense of alignment and commitment. This process has enabled us to internalize high-impact leadership insights. These insights have helped us elevate our game in ways that accelerate business results. Inside it all, the way we have bonded as a team and become energized and unified about our mission is a priceless bonus."

Working with your team is show time. If you say, "Our culture celebrates best ideas regardless of rank," then let's experience it. If you want to build a robust learning and debrief culture, let's practice it and build its muscle memory right now.

If we want to demonstrate outcome-focus, let's exercise its mental model in this conversation right now.

What is culture? What defines it?

Culture is perceived and experienced in:

A. The behaviors we demonstrate at work
B. Our values in action
C. Our social and behavioral "operating system"
D. Our dos and don'ts
E. The stories we tell
F. The heroes we celebrate and emulate
G. The protocols, language, tone, symbols, and rituals we use to communicate and manage our work and expectations.

How does culture relate to our business? Why do we integrate the culture conversation with our exploration?
Culture—our behavioral operating system and the stories we share—conveys to team members:

• What matters and what is rewarded.
• How we get things done.
• Who has decision rights and who is accountable.
• How to respond to a crisis.
• What to do when in doubt.
• How we engage internally and externally with partners and customers.
• What we celebrate and what we reject.
• What risks one should and should not take.
• How to advance in the organization.

To learn about the culture of an organization, I convert these culture characteristics into questions we use in our exploration. For example:

- Who are the exemplars that people learn from and emulate?
- What do they do and how do they get things done?
- What observable behaviors will you see every day at work that best express the culture of the organization?
- What have you celebrated together recently?
- Who has been rewarded recently, and for what kind of behaviors and outcomes?
- What is an example of a crisis you have dealt with? How did you address this challenge? Who was involved? Who had the power to make decisions and drive change? What enabled you to resolve this situation successfully?
- What are the best ways to accelerate priorities in this organization? Who typically gets involved? How do they accelerate the desired resolution?
- How do you work together to move forward the big objectives of the organization? How do you help each other when you face important deadlines?
- In recent times, what has been for you the most exciting day at work? What made it exciting?

Through answers to these questions, I achieve two objectives. First, I gain important insights into the client organization. Second, I facilitate people's own discoveries. We are mining for insights about the culture, what works well, and what the executives are called to change, update, and develop in order to create the future they are seeking.

Critical Culture Pivots

One simple conversation format that elicits new realizations and provokes new insights is the pivot conversation. Consider that a question is a set-up for discovery that unleashes movement. The word "question" implies a "quest for ion"—a quest for energy. A purposeful question can help you access the group's creative potential, and unleash its kinetic energy as people seek its answer.

Unleashing the energy of transformation is what the pivot conversation is about. Its purpose is to discover and bring into focus the behaviors we must demonstrate to create the change we envision. What "from—to" pivots are essential to our success?

Here are a few examples of "from—to" pivots that executive teams have chosen to focus on to catalyze the change they envision. By sharpening their Horizon Two priorities, they are able to build the future state they had described in the Horizon Three vision and strategy exercise (*Portal Seven*).

From	To
Focus on doing our job	Focus on the value we provide
Functional activities	Business outcomes
Silo vision	End-to-end services
Subject matter experts	Solution experts
Complex	Easy
Completing projects	Operationalizing solutions
Defensive engagement	Open and transparent engagement
Data input	Actionable insights
Incremental	Transformational
PowerPoint slide shows	Open and authentic conversations
I ask/you do	Joint "we do" decisions
Accountability alignment	Value alignment
IT-led	Business-led
High touch	Just right to meet individual needs
Descriptive: report what happens	Prescriptive: impact what happens

By asking the managers to reflect on what "from—to" pivots are most essential to success, we facilitate a conversation that produces internal and inter-personal reflections and stimulates movement.

I then ask the team, "What concrete agreements are you prepared to make? What agreements will help you catalyze the organizational future you imagine and are committed to bring to life?"

Here is a sample of such agreements from team members who recently answered these questions:

a. Identify and eliminate non-value added work. If it isn't driving an outcome, stop doing it.
b. Encourage and reward initiative and leadership at all levels.
c. Foster open conversations.
d. Set clear expectations.
e. Offer concrete feedback about observed behaviors and how they help or hinder.
f. Provide air cover for calculated risk-taking.
g. Begin with "Why?" to anchor conversations to desired outcomes.
h. Practice transparent debriefs to foster accelerated learning.
i. Model ownership and enforce accountability.
j. Foster an agile iterative way of working.
k. Convert data into actionable insights.
l. Evaluate end-to-end impact to determine preferred solutions.

The Contribution Pivot

Let's explore another pivot I use to guide a critical shift in mindset and behavior. My coaching interaction with Scott occurred in the midst of a large reorganization in his company. After Scott described his introductory meeting with his new future boss, I responded by saying, "There are three options for your next move. Option one is to wait and do nothing until your new boss gets in touch to let you know your new role has been approved.

"Option two is to send her a quick email saying, 'Cathy, I am looking forward to joining your team and getting started in my new role soon.'

"Option three is to send her an email saying, 'Cathy, I am excited to join your team. You mentioned that you are deliberating the bigger organizational change that is needed. If you would like me to brainstorm with you about the options you are considering, I'd love to be part of that conversation.'"

"I see the options," Scott said, "but it's been three days since the meeting, so I am not sure about the third option."

"In the third option, you promote yourself into a peer conversation and relationship with your new boss, which is an optimal position for you to be in," I offered. "Ideally, the time to open this dialogue was in the moment when she said to you, 'I want to change the nature of the role before I put you into the position. The person who just left the position got burned out in this global responsibility and I'd like to change the scope.' Your response at that moment could have been, 'Do you feel that you diagnosed clearly the cause? I can think of four or five plausible reasons why this role led to a burn out.'

"The point," I added, "is that this would allow you to shift the conversation from *your need* to *her need*. Instead of focusing on *your problem*, which is whether you have a role, you shift the conversation to focus on *her problem*, which is diagnosing the cause of the organizational stress and coming up with the best solution.

"The point of this reframing, Scott, is that when you said to her, 'Is there anything you want me to focus on in the meantime?' you intimated a subordinate relationship. Shifting the focus to her need and suggesting she can brainstorm possible solutions with you would have moved you up the value ladder from a subordinate to a consultative relationship with your boss. That's the best of relationships you can foster."

"I can see this," Scott said. "What I wonder is why did that response not occur to me in the moment?"

"I can answer this question on your behalf by pointing to your education and upbringing where deference to superiors was important. Given the nature of your career, you have focused on being great at execution. The reason you hired me to coach you now was to help you build strategic prowess, executive presence, and charisma in communication. I propose there is a better question you can ask. Instead of wondering why a given approach did not occur to you in the moment, consider this question: what is the inner configuration and thought process that naturally would trigger a consultative response?

"My answer, Scott, is that first you've got to be curious. Second, you must choose to see yourself always as serving the need outside of you. This is about discovering that the best way to serve your need is to focus on the needs of the person you interact with, and explore how you can help bring value to address his or her need. This is the contribution pivot and the thought process that would create this conversation naturally.

"Third, I propose that you reframe the questions most managers focus on, namely, 'What should I do?' and 'How should I respond?' by asking, 'What opportunities are available for me to contribute?' Try to be explorative as a foundational disposition. Although it takes more work on the front end, it often leads to a higher impact response. Generating options is a great step to help you expand your considerations and clarify your thinking."

Resilience

Resilience is the ability to bounce back, pick yourself up and go on.
It is the power to self-heal, renew
and always take the next step forward.
Resilience is in reconnecting with the line of your life and endeavor,
joining it where it has moved to now, not where you left it last.

Resilience has the quality of robustness;
it is the capacity for spontaneous recovery.
The repair, replenishment and recharge
are generated by the will to live and to go on,
and by the determination to take the next step,
to proceed forward.
It is the regeneration of all that can be.

Resilience is another name for life itself,
and for the power of nature to recreate itself.
It is much more than coming back to previous equilibrium.
It is the ability to embrace change and be made new in it,
to seize the new opportunity it brings.

You have seen a toddler moving from crying
to smiling to laughing in seconds—that's resilience.
You've seen how people devastated by an earthquake or a tsunami
pick up and go on with their lives—that's resilience.
You have seen yourself reaching the end of your rope
and your strength,
reaching a point of despair, only to find a new start
and discover a new day,
to move forward again in a new way and with a new power—
that's resilience.

Resilience knows no end. It has no limits and no boundaries.
It is the fountain of life and living,
the absolution that spring brings to winter,
the unstoppable vine of growth, of love, of beauty and of purpose.
It is the hope passed on from one generation to the next,
and the covenant that there shall always be a new day,
and that you, too, always can make a new start.
Embrace your resilience today.
Become the catalyst for the tomorrow you envision.

Building a Future in the Three-Story House of Work

Where we explore a new thinking architecture and a template for action and growth.

A renowned rabbi once said, "We all come to this life to do two kinds of things: what is easiest and what is most difficult for us. The easiest reveal your gifts; they show you what you are meant to be doing. The most difficult challenges teach you to go beyond your self-limiting beliefs; they help you embrace powers greater than your own."

The Three Buckets of Value:
Are You the One Out of Ten?

What separates those who are able to go above and beyond their goals to surprise themselves and others, from those who merely achieve their goals?

The difference results from a choice you and I face daily in small and big ways. This choice is framed in my coaching dialogue with Peter. First, here is a framing context that I apply in a variety of coaching situations.

I proposed earlier that the work of leadership is connecting and framing conversations, specifically, conversations that mobilize action. In the coaching with Peter, I use the "three buckets" framing technique to facilitate forward movement and advance his decision process by creating distinctions among differing levels of response.

The three buckets provide an easy framework to help shift an unfocused discussion into an exploration that examines alternatives and moves the action forward.

I also use the three framing buckets to:
a. Differentiate three kinds of categories.
b. Establish three levels (altitudes) of looking at a problem.
c. Separate a complex situation into three buckets of issues.
d. Describe three octaves of process that influence each other.
e. Define three buckets of value.

Here is how I describe the three buckets of value that executives can expect to experience as a result of our collaboration. "The future we are creating together with teams and organizations begins by framing the benefits and value we will produce in our joint effort." By setting high expectations that we are committed to and accountable for, we set the stage for an accelerated journey forward.

The first bucket of value involves the company. We deliver dramatic value that significantly impacts business results. This is the foreground focus and the context of our work. "If our collaboration does not impact your business and meaningfully improve your results," I tell executives, "we lose the business rationale for our work, even when the other two buckets provide great value. On the other hand, impacting your business without creating the second and third buckets of value is unsatisfactory and is a missed opportunity."

My ambition and aspiration are to create additional value for the organization by impacting the team and every individual present. These are buckets two and three.

The second bucket is about creating value for the team. Why do we form working teams? The simple answer is that to realize your mission and create the future you imagine requires the skills and capabilities of many people working collaboratively. One person alone cannot achieve these ambitious results. Each person brings to the table their strengths and weaknesses, and no one individual carries full-spectrum mission-critical knowhow. Good teams appreciate and promote each other's strengths; they guard against blind spots and counteract weaknesses by balancing them with the strengths. Therefore, I impact the team by creating bucket two value.

There are too many teams of brilliant people who, rather than produce collective wisdom, generate collective stupidity, and even collective breakdowns that lead to disastrous outcomes. Therefore, I design the team dimension of our work to help its members step up to a whole new operating level and build a learning culture that avoids self-inflicting calamities. That is the second bucket of value.

The third bucket of value concerns the individuals. I know for a fact that I will learn and grow through the experience of my interaction with any team. I aspire to help the managers also grow through the experience by gaining new self-insight and appreciation of their own strengths, and by building new skills, capabilities, and executive presence. That is the third bucket of value.

Three Buckets of Value

Bucket One
Company—deliver dramatic business results

Bucket Two
Team—develop a sustainable culture of initiative
and accountability

Bucket Three
Personal—enhance managers' effectiveness
and executive presence

Insight:

The number three (3) is central to the blueprint of life. It lends itself to powerful and intuitive frameworks because threes appear in almost everything you see.

Consider that most of what we look at and deal with is influenced by the following dynamics:
• Past—present—future
• Beginning—middle—end
• Awake—twilight zone—asleep
• Conscious—semi-conscious—unconscious
• Birth—life—death
• Inhale—extract—exhale
• Mother—father—child
• High pressure—low pressure—movement
• Bottom—top—space between
• Increase—balance—decrease
• Coming—pausing—going

You get the idea...

Practice application:

• How can you view a problem you are working on right now with new eyes by applying the three buckets framing technique?

I apply the three buckets as a framing tool in my conversation with Peter to differentiate categories and provide him with a defined choice point. In this case the conversation is about his personal development agenda in the context of career development.

Peter is a talented manager. Because he tends to be understated, his demeanor can hide his talent and intelligence. Here is how our coaching conversation about his professional development unfolded, and how I used the three buckets to help Peter turn his deliberations into forward action.

Peter: "The feedback from my boss confirms that she is pleased with the significant progress I've made with my team in achieving our goals. To demonstrate that I am a strong candidate for the next level executive role, she proposed that I pursue three growth opportunities:

1. Become a more assertive driver and closer.
2. Be the 'bigger person' by taking the initiative, presenting my point of view, leading the conversation, and stepping up to challenges by re-framing setbacks as opportunities.
3. Accelerate my project work by bringing issues to closure more quickly.

"How would you advise me to approach these suggestions?"

"Well, Peter, your boss has given you very specific and concrete feedback. You now are at a crossroads: rest on your laurels and ignore the opportunities, or rise to the challenge to build on your achievements and improve your performance."

Peter's reply was immediate. "I definitely want to apply myself in these opportunity areas."

"Congratulations! Do you realize that by making this one simple decision to take action, you have separated yourself from 50% of people in the workforce? Let me explain by putting your choice into context."

Here is the context I described. Out of every ten people in the workforce, five are doing nothing about their development and growth. They merely are reacting, coasting, or even drifting from day to day without the focus of a development agenda. This paradigm says, "I am coming here to do a job. Do not ask me to do more than that." It is shocking that 50% of employees bring no self-directed focus to their personal growth, failing to recognize that the work environment itself presents a fantastic development opportunity.

Four people out of ten choose to embrace the mental

model of development and growth. They build on their core strengths and previous successes, augmenting and capitalizing on behaviors and skills that already have delivered dividends for them. Frankly, this is a smart approach. Why? We know that we learn best and fastest by expanding from our core strengths, by applying the virtuous cycle of success and positive experience, and by doing more of what we do well. We also know that it is easier to elevate good performance to excellent performance than it is to convert bad performance to mediocre performance. That, in a nutshell, is the strengths-based approach to development. Sadly, many people stop their personal development journey at this point. However, it is not the end of the road. To continue the journey from here requires a different choice.

Only one person in ten decides to go beyond the strengths-based approach to personal development. These individuals essentially are saying in their own ways, "I intend to challenge myself to proactively and strategically seek opportunities that catalyze my growth and development." That is the one-in-ten choice. It is driven by entrepreneurial energy that is not content with the status quo. The one-in-ten person believes that staying in place actually is going backwards, and therefore is restless enough to generate movement that expands into the unknown and the uncertain.

I draw the three buckets here to elucidate the point of this thinking frame:

Three attitudes toward personal growth in the workplace

Coast or react

Grow from strength

Grow beyond the comfort zone

"Which bucket represents your choice, Peter?

"You can decide to follow the well-trodden path of those who decide to join the 'four in ten' group, or you can opt to take the path less traveled, the one chosen by the 'one in ten' group. The difference between the people in these two groups is that those in the latter recognize that certain experiences are acquired only when you seriously challenge yourself. The 'one in ten' choice implies exposing yourself to situations that require you to operate outside your comfort zone. It is a choice to embrace growth opportunities that at times push you against your natural inclination and a declaration of readiness to take the initiative, and navigate in uncertain terrains where the rewards can be significant, though success is not guaranteed.

"What's the unifying denominator for the 'one in ten' professionals?

"In my experience, what differentiates the 'one in ten' is that they are self-starters, driven from the inside out. Although they embrace external stimuli when available, they are not dependent on them for their growth. They love learning and growing more than they love the safety of playing only on their home turf."

"If I don't challenge myself out of my comfort zone, I get bored," Peter observed.

"That mindset determines how you approach your growth and development plan. I respect your choice, Peter. As your trusted adviser, I would not be critical if you had said, 'Life is good, and I am happy to be in the four-in-ten group for now.' However, I would point out that engaging me to help you as a leader inside that context may be a misallocation of resources. Your decision validates the point of our work together. We now can bring laser focus to your opportunities and develop a concrete action plan so that both of us can hold you accountable."

At this point, our conversation shifted to address the three growth opportunities Peter decided to embrace. Peter's aptitude and eagerness to embrace discomfort and risk provided a broader range of alternative strategies and tactics for him to deploy. He was carving out his own one-in-ten path.

Practice application:

- What steps are you taking to create your professional future?

- How proactive and strategic are you in setting your personal development goals and pursuing your vision for yourself?

- What competencies and skills are you developing at this moment? How will they help you achieve the future you envision?

Diagnostic Dexterity: What Problem Are You Trying to Solve?

Tim did not sound his usual self. His weaker voice revealed disappointment and sense of letdown. "I am worried that my team is not motivated to embrace our expanded mission and climb the next mountain in front of us."

"What is the reason for your worry? What evidence do you have that they are not motivated?" I asked.

"Well, our kick-off meeting yesterday was not as exciting or energizing as I had expected. Some people were focused on minor details, while others did not engage in the conversation at all. I did not get the feeling that our team is embracing the future we are trying to create."

"I understand, Tim, and I can visualize the picture of your meeting. Have you considered the possibility that you are diagnosing your team's response incorrectly? Is it plausible that what you call lack of motivation is a case of displaced diagnostic?"

"What do you mean by 'displaced diagnostic'? Our meeting obviously lacked energy and a sense of motivation to move forward."

I proceeded to make the following two points. "First, unless you diagnose the problem you are trying to solve correctly, you are unlikely to implement an effective intervention. Second, the danger in displaced analysis is that trying to solve the wrong problem, or one that does not exist, will cause you to miss the problem at hand.

"In your situation, I can think of four possible reasons why you felt your team's lack of motivation. Before we explore these, tell me why people fail to analyze situations correctly. What do you think is the main cause for displaced analysis?"

"Well, I'd imagine that it is a lack of information."

"Although insufficient information may be one of the symptoms, it is not the main cause. In my observation, Tim, intellectual laziness and lack of curiosity are more often the reasons people fail to appreciate and analyze their situations correctly. Often it takes work to identify the cause of a given problem. When you practice diagnostic thinking and make plausible cause distinctions, you will stand out for the clarity you bring, and for doing work that others prefer to not pick up. Many people find it easier to stay at a superficial level of analysis. It provides them with an alibi for not initiating change, and excuses their failure to create the desired new future."

Tim laughed. "I see this kind of laziness at work every day. But we don't want to be lazy here, so let us get to the point." Smiling confidently, he proceeded, "What are the four possible factors I lazily mischaracterized as lack of motivation?"

"Well, the first possibility is that people are not excited because they do not see the same future that you do. Ask yourself, 'Have I painted a clear and compelling picture of the future, one that clearly outlines what success will look like?'

"The second possibility is that you have painted a clear picture at a high level but have not communicated clearly that each person has a personal opportunity within the future state. In this case, your team may understand the picture of the expanded mission at a high conceptual level, but it's evident they don't realize yet that each individual can contribute to its achievement.

"The third possibility as to why your team seems to lack motivation is, while they do understand the big picture and see their individual contributions, they don't believe they have the tools or capabilities to realize their opportunities. Ask yourself, 'Have we provided people with the tools and capabilities to address the opportunities before us?' If they do not feel competently ready, the opportunity becomes a source of anxiety rather than of excitement.

"The fourth possibility is that they have the tools, but given their other projects, they are uncertain about priorities. In this case, the question to reflect on is, 'Have we established a clear sense of priorities? Have we clarified what we will de-prioritize, or remove altogether from the current activity map, to make space for the new work?'

"So, Tim, which of the four possibilities is it?"

"I think it is number three and number four," Tim offered. "It is quite clear now what my next actions must be this week. I will follow up individually with team members to find out exactly what concerns them, so that I address the right problem."

Insight:

• To implement an effective solution, make sure you are clear about the problem you are trying to solve.

Practice application:

• Ask yourself these three questions:

1. What problem are we trying to solve?
2. What evidence supports our analysis?
3. What other plausible reasons could explain the symptoms we have observed?

Correct diagnosis begins by distinguishing between what is not the problem, and what is the problem. For example, emergency room medicine is not about discovering what you have, but about ruling out a series of life threatening scenarios.

The Three Minds and My Net-casting End of the Year Envisioning

In your personal and career planning, the competencies you choose to develop are only one element inside a bigger picture that makes up the holistic architecture of your life.

Most large companies have an established annual planning process that often is driven by the Chief Financial Officer and constrained by budgetary requirements. Their preferred scenario is one in which business units as well as the company as a whole instigate a three horizons strategy and envisioning process that is not defined by the annual budget planning. As discussed earlier, a strategy is a process that begins by identifying the desired future and working backwards. In contrast, a planning process extrapolates the current state into the future. We actually need to consider both approaches. However, the risk is that the tactical planning process takes over the strategy conversation. When you let Horizon One (and horizon 0) tactical urgency hijack the strategy, you may arrive very efficiently at the wrong place. In my mental model, optimizing the altitude of your flight to reduce fuel burnout (tactics) cannot replace establishing clarity about the destination of your flight (strategy).

As is the case with your business and with your career path, you want to establish your envisioning and planning processes for your whole life. In our case, Sara and I run our consulting business in a way that allows us to integrate our work around our lifestyle. Because I can work wherever we are, we spend the summer in Seattle and the winter in Jupiter, Florida.

Every season and every new year bring a flux of growth opportunities and challenges, as well as the energy to address both. Each year, I engage in imagining and creating a space for next new possibility horizons. In October I begin to "cast the net" for the coming year. It's a great time to focus, reflect, explore ideas, and deliberate about options. I use this annual net casting to bring myself up to date on all aspects of my work and life.

What do I include in this annual reflective exploration?

I harvest learning from my journey to date, and I identify needs, trends, and directions. I draw up future plans and possibilities. Although this process begins in October, I continue it through the end of the year. Building layer upon layer of insights helps me cast a wider net. It provides time to breathe in and out the full scope of work and life, to capture ideas, connect the dots and distill new intelligence.

This net-casting deliberation includes reflecting on specific questions. Some of them need time to simmer and percolate to engage the full spectrum of insights available within the three speeds of the mind.

What are the three speeds of the mind? Here is how I would describe them, along with the fourth mind, which is the reflective mindful mind.

Bringing forward the best insights, wisdom, and ideas requires the engagement of your whole mind—the Snap Mind, the Ponder Mind and the Weaver Mind. A fourth mind, the Self-reflective Mind, oversees the other three and purposefully allocates and directs attention where it sees fit. The Self-reflective Mind is asleep most of the time; when awake, it moves into self-surveillance mode and listens. Then it offers diagnostic value and calibrates your focus as you engage your three mind speeds.

1. Snap is your fast mind.
It delivers quick, in-the-moment judgments about the situations you encounter. The Snap is the biological product of evolution and the need for survival. It often is referred to as a "gut" or "instinctive" response. Although you always should listen to and hear the Snap Mind, you must be discerning and analyze

its conclusions before deciding whether to act on them. Be curious about the information it delivers. Do not dismiss or suppress the snap insight. Unless faced with life threatening conditions, you would be well advised to engage the Ponder Mind and the Weaver Mind before you take action.

2. Ponder is your medium-speed mind.
You engage the Ponder Mind when you say, "Let me sleep on this." Delaying an immediate decision is one way to activate the Ponder Mind, which summons additional intelligence and insight because it involves your semi-conscious and unconscious processes. By nature, the pondering process is slower than the snap instinct. Your Ponder Mind forms a picture that previously was not visible by tapping into your latent intuition to connect seemingly unrelated data points. It is the knowing sense you get the following morning or a couple of days after you initially consider an issue, when suddenly you have a clear sense of what options are good and which are not.

The Ponder Mind delivers ideas when you are not focusing squarely on a problem, such as when you are in the shower, or running, or watching TV. This mind works best when you are working on a question or set of questions that you have seeded in your semi-conscious filing system. The envisioning cast-up process at the end of the year is a good time to deliberately engage the Ponder Mind.

3. The Weaver is your slower mind.
The Weaver Mind is responsible for helping you perform your due diligence by analyzing situations thoroughly. The function of the Weaver Mind is to engage in thorough deliberation, to map all parts and to activate your analytical study and thinking. Weaving involves interlacing two sets of threads—warp and weft. The Weaver Mind integrates opportunities and challenges. It meshes content and form, input and desired outcome; it weighs options and risk-reward ratios. Your loom is the framework you create for the Weaver Mind, which loves process formats that enable thorough evaluation.

When you identify what opportunities are available to you in the near term and envision those you intend to create within the three and five years' horizons, you weave a larger net when you call upon these three minds. Casting this wider net enables golden opportunities to find you more readily and easily.

> Insight:
>
> • Creating a new future requires the three minds—the Snap, the Ponder and the Weaver—as well as the Self-reflective mind. All these elements must be part of our conversation.

Your Three-story House

How do you open new portals into the future? What creates the future?

Development creates the future. Growing and evolving as individuals and as teams create new futures. The work of purpose and innovation creates new portals into the future. Focus, intention, overcoming challenges and setbacks, love, compassion, resilience, and optimism all are thresholds of possibility into a new future. Daring to take risks, trying new activities, and seeking new learning all contribute to creating the future.

How do we facilitate and engender these future-making processes?

Conversation is the oxygen that enables development, growth, and the work of purpose and innovation. The conversations you develop are your portals into tomorrow. They unleash new powers that can create different and new futures.

To help Peter realize his opportunities, our coaching dialogue explored the different levels of his inquiry. The initial triggers were his career and his work. But work never occurs at just one level. I disagree with the movie character Forest Gump: life is not like a box of chocolates—life is like a three-story house. The Three-story House is a framework I introduce to foster the thinking that unleashes new growth potential. Here is how I use it.

Imagine that on each floor of your metaphoric three-story house you perform a different kind of work. Most people confine themselves to the first floor. Some people climb to the second floor. Very rarely, a few make it to the third floor.

To understand what takes place in your three stories of work, let's look at each of these spaces. The first floor is where you work *in* the business. It is a busy place. You spend many of your hours working in the business.

On the second floor you work *on* the business. Notice the distinction between working *in* and working *on* the business. You work *in the business* to serve your clients; you work *on the business* to improve the business operation.

When you climb to the third floor, there is a different kind of work to do. The third floor is where you work *on you*. You are your most important tool: your capabilities, your energy, and your beliefs determine what you are able to produce when you work *on the business* on the second floor, and *in the business* on the ground floor.

Unleashing the fullest growth potential of your life and your business requires that you work on all three floors. As a leader, for example, you coach your teams to improve their execution and service to customers (first floor), you optimize work processes (second floor), and you build your own capabilities, resilience, and confidence (third floor).

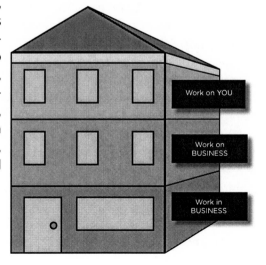

From Impossibility to Graceful Action

As a leader of a global team, Don was asked by the COO to develop and implement a new set of go-to-market and marketing strategies to facilitate entry into new markets and to stimulate growth in existing markets. The company's culture is initiative-based, and he has broad flexibility for shaping his approach to his work objectives. Don is a smart executive with keen intuition and a creative flare. Occasionally he tends to insert unnecessary complexity into his work. His ability to process huge volumes of data enables him to absorb endless input and feedback.

Don was excited to have a role that enables him to be a catalyst for innovation. At the same time, he was concerned about the company's ecosystem. As Don explained the situation, he was asked to create new outcomes while maneuvering the complex and political environment of a matrix organization that is grounded in a legacy and protocols that hinder his task.

Where do you begin? How do you navigate complex environments to create breakthrough results? These were the questions Don was grappling with when he asked for my help.

Our first conversation explored Don's opportunities to create momentous progress. This conversation took place on the second floor of our metaphoric three-story house. On this floor we evaluated his organizational strategy and redesigned his roadmap. Don had been working with his team on the first floor to execute the organization's strategy. To enter a reflective space and enable new thinking, we explored a range of "second floor" type questions. The resulting conversations help re-imagine how work gets done on the first floor.

When we met again, Don seemed almost a different person. Immersed in and overwhelmed by the challenges presented by the business and by the expectations of senior leaders, he carried the weight of many concerns on his shoulders. In part, he was struggling with factors that were outside his control. Delivering in-the-business results (first floor) required the support and approval of his boss, whom Don experienced as unresponsive and somewhat erratic. At times, his boss would take a deep interest in Don's work, only to disappear suddenly, leaving Don to initiate movement on matters that required the boss's involvement.

This spaghetti bowl of concerns Don was cooking soon spilled out onto the table. I re-introduced the three-story house metaphor to help him name, separate and sort the issues. Here is the process I use to build the conversation menu and discover the path of highest energy potential.

First I asked Don to do a download off the top of his head of all his concerns. I made a list.

Second, we examined each issue one by one. I asked Don to give me two inputs on each of the 14 items on the list. The first was an assessment of the urgency and intensity of the issue using a one-through-ten scale, with ten implying the issue had reached a boiling point, and one indicating minimal concern. The second input was a brief explanation of why the issue mattered, and how, if at all, it was critical to his success.

Writing the issue and urgency scale next to the image of the house, I used Don's context and reasoning to suggest on which of the three floors to place each concern. Gradually we developed and prioritized a complete agenda of topics to address. One of the issues Don described related to his boss. Based on a few odd comments, he had inferred and extrapolated a picture of his standing with his boss. He was concerned that the perceived lack of support from his boss would have a negative impact on his ability to produce the desired results. Don's tone, energy, and narrative revealed how he had tied himself up in knots about this situation.

To Don's first floor list of bullets I added:

• Priorities: How will I bring focus to a few of our vital priorities?
• Momentum: How will we create rapid wins to build credibility and momentous movement, and help us create a coalition of support?

I proposed adding these questions to the second floor menu:

- Managing up: What alternatives are available for me to engage my boss so I can gain the support I need to be successful?
- Managing down: What will help my team climb this next mountain? How will I utilize our time together to build an inspirational work environment and engender rigor and accountability?

I captured the following bullets for the third floor agenda:

- Why do I feel off center? Do I feel that my work is appreciated? Do I feel that I am valued? How do these concerns impact my work?
- In what situations do I respond from a scarcity mindset? Why? When do I access an abundance frame of mind? What helps me operate from this center of gravity? How do my self-esteem and self-talk reflect these mindsets?

During our third floor conversation, Don reflected on his beliefs and the mental models that had shaped his operating system to understand how and why he responded to situations the way he did. He wondered what internal activity pathways turned on as he worked to achieve results. To promote his self-awareness by bringing the background to the foreground, I used questions such as, "Why is this important?" and, "Why do you believe this to be the case?"

These types of inquiries facilitated the discovery and self-awareness that was necessary for Don to take pragmatic action, such as building a coalition of support for his initiatives by cultivating his stakeholders.

Don's "third-floor" awareness and insights, along with his reflection on what was working well and what could sabotage his management impact, led him to realize how he could do a better job of eliciting the best in each of his talented team members. We proceeded through the list, prioritizing and planning the next phase of Don's strategy to build a broader coalition of support and catalyze movement.

What happened through this conversation validates the value of emergent conversations that follow the energy potential. I observed a shift in Don as we explored his menu of topics, asking the "why" questions (third floor), the "what" questions (second floor), and the "how" questions (first floor), and distilling his vital priorities and actions. By externalizing his process and re-framing his concerns within a new thinking architecture that provided clarity, his stress and worry backed off. Don looked refreshed, energized and ready to make his next moves. Using the three-story house framework to guide his reflections and actions, he experienced great relief as the convoluted was untangled, the impossible became doable, and stagnation gave way to forward movement.

During our debrief, Don explained, "Our thoughts create our actions. By clarifying my thinking, I am able to bring clarity to my actions. As a result, I am able to eliminate noise and radically accelerate my process. On the first floor I tend to be reactive. This can get exhaustingly frustrating for me, and even more so for my team. By going to the second floor, I become centered in my control field. I then find the clarity of focus that helps me build my influence with my peers as well as with my boss and other senior leaders of the company. By working *on my work*, not just *in my work*, I dramatically improve our results. An even greater uplift occurs when I release what holds me back by reframing third floor concerns. From this sense of clarity emerges graceful action."

A Theater of Opportunity to Express Your Talent

Don is not the only executive to describe this kind of trans-formation. I observe this phenomenon when I engage other executives in a similar process. Movement is unleashed when clarity dispels the fog of confusion. By applying architecture thinking—the three-stories of work—we facilitate a new level of intelligence and actionable insights about the present state, and about the new futures we can enable.

The first floor is where Don works *in his job*.
The second floor is where he works *on his job*.
The third floor is where Don works *on himself* and his "inner operating system."

The challenges are different at each of these three levels. The power to catalyze movement and transform your results is found in attending to the needs and opportunities at each level. This process helps executives escape the industrial mechanistic view of their work, where humans sometimes are viewed almost as robotic production units.

Creative brilliance is found and unleashed by embracing and re-integrating who we are as humans into our work. Re-integrating our humanness allows us to see work as an opportunity theater to discover our talents and facilitate our growth.

Naturally, busy executives are preoccupied with working in the business (first floor), and managing and optimizing the business (second floor). In the course of our collaboration, Don discovered he gets his best ideas when he works in parallel, going up and down all three stories as necessary.

Don reflected, "By developing awareness of my strengths and leadership voice, and understanding how I learn best and produce results, I am more effective and strategic in how I apply myself to the business. I am able to reframe issues more effectively and personalize my communication. This outcome is eye-opening. What was mostly in the background has moved into the foreground. The dramatic results we've achieved are a testament to the impact this framework has had in changing how I do my work, and how our team operates."

Practice application:

- To develop the three-story thinking about your business, consider the following:

Level	Imperatives	Key Questions
Ground floor Working *in* the business	• Deliver value to clients • Grow the business • Preserve service quality	• Who are your clients? • What are their unmet needs? • How will you delight clients? • Who else can you help?
Second floor Working *on* the business	Improve strategic effectiveness and operational efficiency	• What is the future picture of your business? • What must be true for your desired future to play out? • What is your prioritization process? • In what ways do you need to pivot?
Top floor Working *on* you	• Develop you • Live into purpose	• What inspires you? • What concerns must you address? • What new capabilities will you develop? • How do you lead your teams to build purpose-inspired action?

Portal 12

Champions, Presence, and What Matters

Where we discover the 72-hour rule and the "half full" insight.

Chris was a good engineer, one of a dozen on his team who answered service calls. Methodical and thorough, Chris was well respected by his team members. He was not the star type—quiet, a little shy, never seeking center stage; Chris's focus was on the task at hand.

High performance creates its own growth. As a result of its service quality, the team took ownership of a new service contract. Jed was the chief contact on the client's end. Within a couple of weeks, it became clear that Jed was a demanding and extremely difficult individual. Every Tuesday or Wednesday, without exception, the phone would ring and Jed would be on the line, sometimes even twice a week. Impatient, angry, and thankless, he did not make his calls easy on the team, who experienced them as abusive and obnoxious. Jed was "burning" one engineer after another. Within a few weeks, almost no one wanted to take his calls. When people heard his voice, they immediately transferred the call to Chris, who remained the only person on the team ready and willing to service Jed's needs. He would reply patiently, talk Jed through the technical issues and resolve every problem presented. Chris never seemed to get offended or upset with Jed's demeanor. He would calmly solve the problem and move on. Chris quickly became legendary for his ability to handle the company's most difficult client. Over time, Jed gradually began to change. Though he continued to be unpleasant, he seemed to respect and like Chris, even though he remained difficult for everyone else to handle.

"How can you be so understanding and patient with such an abusive client?" Chris was asked. His reply, "Every time I take the call, I remind myself that I have to deal with this man for twenty or thirty minutes, but he has to deal with himself all day long, seven days a week. This thought immediately fills me with compassion."

Chris's insight is that in many situations, people's frustration and anger are an expression of their own pain and struggle. In most instances such people are not against you; they simply struggle to live with themselves. Have compassion for them; they must live with themselves all the time. If they behave with you as Jed did with the service team, they likely find it very difficult to live with themselves. Be thankful you live with you.

Opportunities Have Expiration Dates

By recognizing that an opportunity emerges inside a WOO (window of opportunity), we imply that it shows up with an expiration date.

We get up in the morning hoping for the best to find us. We each have a unique picture of our idealized future. We each include in this picture the elements we consider important. For example, you might hope to encounter situations that open doors for you to grow, to improve, to be promoted, to acquire new knowledge, to meet new people, and to discover new latent capabilities.

These opportunities appear inside limited situational windows and do not exist in a void. What do I mean by expiration date? If you spot an opportunity inside its window, anything can become possible. Outside its window, that opportunity ceases to exist, or its return-on-potential diminishes rapidly.

Think about an airport terminal. You arrive on one flight and you must catch a connecting flight to reach your final destination. The window is defined by the space between the time of arrival and departure. It is like this in business and in life. There are narrow windows of opportunity before the next departure. The question is, will you catch the connecting flight to your next destination?

Will your business, your team, catch the next departure?

Business is full of examples of missed windows of opportunity. For example, both Nokia and Blackberry failed to spot a new departure in the evolution of smart phones. Kodak invented the digital camera, but by suppressing its development, the company missed its window of opportunity and ultimately went out of business. Yahoo, one of the early success stories of the Internet, surrendered the "search business" to the primacy of Google because it missed a series of windows.

Microsoft led the "personal computer window" with its "Windows" operating system. It was so successful in that space, however, that it missed the early stages of the Internet and the "search window." In early 2008, Microsoft offered to acquire Yahoo for close to $45 billion. Jerry Yang, Yahoo's co-founder and then CEO, said the bid "substantially undervalued Yahoo." Eight years later, Verizon acquired Yahoo for $4.8 billion, making Yang's decision a catastrophic miscalculation! Microsoft also failed to see the next series of big windows, such as the "mobile window" that occurred with the transition to smart phones, and the iPhone phenomenon. The company tried to rectify that failure by spending $7.2 billion to acquire Nokia, only to write it off later as a poor investment. After missing the "social network window," Microsoft sought to catch up by acquiring LinkedIn for $26.2 billion. If these examples are not enough to recognize the critical importance of windows of opportunity, consider that Microsoft nearly missed the "cloud window," the transition of digital services to the cloud. As I write this in 2016, Microsoft is working hard to win market share with Azure, its integrated cloud platform.

What is the lesson here? What can we learn from the missteps of these great companies populated with very smart people who get paid handsomely to identify, respond to, and leverage opportunity windows? The obvious point is that the rear view is a much easier perspective than seeing around the corner. Foresight is rare, and agile responsiveness to an emerging new future is almost as infrequent. This is especially true when you are successful and invested in a cash-rich business model that blinds your vision.

Practice application:

Reflect on important crossroads you have faced:
- What are the important windows of opportunity that have shaped your journey?
- How did you identify them? How did you respond to them?
- What directional decisions did you make at these crossroads that shaped your journey?
- Who influenced you at these critical windows?
- How did you arrange yourself to adapt well through the transition windows?

What is the invisible, perhaps mystical, side of the opportunity windows?

As you seek opportunities, they often find you. It's a two-way, hide-and-seek game of attraction. If you are ready to rise to the occasion and meet the opportunity inside its window, its potential is revealed and expressed.

Champions Are Angels in Disguise

How do opportunities make themselves known? Through people and their conversations.

Twelve executives are in the room with me at the San Francisco Marriott's American Management Association (AMA) center. Sam Szteinbaum leads the North American Consumer group for Hewlett-Packard. The other executives come from a variety of organizations, some from Fortune 100 companies, a few from smaller businesses, and three who are in senior roles at government agencies. They are here to participate in an Executive Effectiveness course, where for five days they will engage in an introspective journey to discover their purpose and articulate their core values.

I've been teaching the Executive Effectiveness course for the AMA for a couple of years and have pushed the program's envelope by "playing jazz" with the process choreography to produce the most memorable experience possible. As a result of my creativity, someone in the AMA subsequently decided to discontinue my instructor contract for that course. Apparently I had pushed the envelope too much.

To facilitate a discovery process where executives imagine the future they want to create, I include a guided imagery exercise, during which participants relax in a foot spa. With the help of my co-conspirator at the Marriott, I've arranged for buckets of warm water to be brought into the room at exactly the right moment on the third morning. I ask people to imagine a joyful day five years in the future: "Given the values and purpose you've been articulating, what is happening during this day five years from now that enables you to express your values and purpose? What else do you do on that day that fills your life with energy and meaning?"

The program unfolds with rich conversations and significant personal breakthroughs all week long. As we wrap up on the last day, Sam approaches me with a question. "Do you think you could HP this for me?"

Of course there is only one answer to a question like this. "Yes, sure," I say. "What do you mean 'HP this for you'?"

"Well, could you do the five-day program in three days?"

"How about if I customize a three-day program for your team that will be even better and more powerful than this experience?"

Six weeks later I facilitate the program for Sam and his team.

"I've been working with some of the people on this team for 16 years, yet in some cases I have learned more about them over the last three days than I had in all these years," says

Bob during our closing circle. The leadership team feedback is positive, and Sam asks me to develop a series of talent programs for his broader organization. Word gets out, and other HP executives call me to conduct our Blue Belt and Silver Belt leadership programs for their teams. Every seminar program promotes new opportunities and sells the next program. The wow multiplier in action generates the referral stories.

Mark Hurd, HP's CEO, asks Sam to take on the Chief Learning Officer position to bring his business savvy to the role and upgrade the company's learning and development function. One opportunity window leads to another. Having a champion in the Chief Learning Officer of a Fortune 20 company when you develop a solo consulting practice is a rare window of opportunity. I get to help HP teams all around the world.

What can we learn from this story about creating new futures? What is the future made of?

The future is made of successive opportunities others help us seize. We all are agents of future possibility to each other. We have become who we are thanks to the million and one small gestures of good will, support, and kindness of total strangers as well as from true champions. My consulting with HP teams continues to this day, 13 years after my initial meeting with Sam.

Executive Presence

In my conversation with Peter (*Portal Eleven*), we separated the one-out-of-ten initiative from the four-out-of-ten response. The one-out-of-ten bucket represents professionals who strive to grow by embracing challenge and expanding beyond the comfort of growing from their strengths. They are champion learners who treat life as an adventure and always are ready to enter a new learning portal that opens the way to a fresh set of possibilities.

My working assumption with top talent groups is that they are in the one-out-of-ten category. What about you? Are you as eager today for your growth as you were when you started your professional journey? Are you as curious and hungry for learning?

Diminished curiosity is the beginning of decline. If you are not developing as a person and a leader, you run the risk of becoming stale and losing interest.

"What is your top development objective as you look forward to the next three years?" was the question I asked a group of top talent managers who came together to work on their personal and career development plans.

First, they reflected on the three-story house framework to identify their priorities. As described earlier, the first floor is where you work in the business, the second floor is where you work on the business, and the third floor is where you work on you.

After they developed their priorities on each of these floors, we opened our coaching forum to give each person an opportunity to dialogue with me about his top goals in front of his peers. The coaching forum provides great learning value as people are able both to experience the dialogue "hot seat" and to learn as their colleagues take their turns.

"My top objective is to develop executive presence," said Tom. He was clear and focused, and his statement was captivating. It was evident he had thought hard about this issue, and his choice to focus on developing executive presence represented a true need.

There is a difference between a true need and a contrived need. A contrived need is one that is adopted or prompted because it sounds right or is fashionable. True need appears from the inside out. As a coach who practices level four listening, I can sense when the person I am working with is speaking from a place of true need. I discern the energy potential, the "electricity," and instantly know that what is said represents a delicious opportunity.

"Developing executive presence is a great goal. Your ability to actualize your goal is as good as your ability to identify the components of executive presence and to develop a concrete plan to build these components," I replied.

Tom did not hesitate. He immediately applied himself to the challenge, thinking out loud about what constitutes executive presence. That is what I love about working with go-getters—their impetus is never about being perfect; rather, they demonstrate the immediacy of self-application. Great learners are people who never stop applying themselves to the next challenge. This is how they grow and differentiate themselves. They see the opportunity portal and walk through it, curious to discover where it takes them. They use the learning impetus to build the momentum of their work and progress.

As my dialogue with Tom evolved, I distilled what I call the "three Vs" framework—the three-legged stool of executive presence. I proposed that Tom focus on these three learnable skills and capacities to guide his plan to cultivate executive presence.

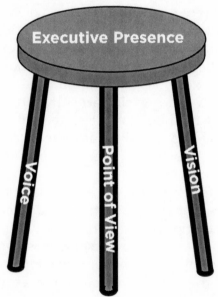

Voice: Finding your voice is the first leg. People pay attention when they feel that you speak in your own voice. Knowledge is power, and the greatest power in the world is self-knowledge. Getting to know yourself and finding your voice is the first leg of executive presence.

Without authenticity, there can be no presence. If you do not know yourself, and do not have the courage to show who you are, if you do not identify and master your strengths, there is no foundation upon which to build executive presence.

Point of View: Developing a point of view is the second leg. To capture your audience's attention, you must bring a unique perspective, an insight that adds value, a position and a point of view that clarify options. You equip your listeners with new understandings and ways of looking at a problem, you frame distinct alternatives, and you offer your recommendations. People know what you value by what you bring to a point of focus. These contributions build your executive presence.

If you offer no new insight, add no new distinction, play it safe, or conceal your point of view for the sake of political correctness, people will tune you out. Executive presence is built by engaging the minds of people and by leading to a point of focus. The interest and engagement of your team augment your presence.

Vision: Painting a vision is the third leg. You describe a picture of the future that pulls others in that direction. You tell a story that is inclusive, you address the needs and interests of the people around the table, and you offer a path forward opening up possibilities they have not considered before. You see a future, or a series of futures, and you are able to share them with others in a convincing way.

If you offer no direction for movement, there will be no energy potential and no presence. Executive presence manifests at the point where insight is translated into action, and where people are compelled to realize the future you describe.

Presence arises from your intent. My proposal for Tom was to develop the three legs of voice, point of view, and vision as part of his plan to cultivate executive presence. The intentionality you express in your voice, your point of view, and your vision is how you build your presence.

The 72-Hour Rule

I learn fastest by teaching and coaching. These types of interactions force me to clarify my thinking and be fully present. Observing a leadership team apply its experience to connect ideas, solve problems, and make decisions is the best learning laboratory in the world. Here is how I stumbled upon the 72-hour rule.

The insights from Justin's and Rob's stories teach us what great learners and leaders do, and reveal how high performers engage in growth opportunities, sometimes surprising themselves and the people around them.

Rob and Justin were bright sales managers, energetic and highly engaged. Two weeks after our workshop, I was puzzled to hear that they had produced very different results. A thorough debriefing of how each one had applied his learning resolved the mystery, and explained the reason for the wide difference in their results.

While Rob was excited about the many new ideas he had heard during our workshop, he still was thinking about the possibilities he had envisioned, without having taken action on the new insights. Justin, on the other hand, had implemented three definitive ideas immediately. After prioritizing a series of concrete steps, he was on his way to exceeding his sales goals.

Comparing Justin's and Rob's actions and their results with the team inspired the formulation of the 72-hour rule.

The 72-hour rule states that if you do not take the first step toward applying a new learning and idea within the first 72 hours, the likelihood that you will implement it quickly approaches zero. Here is what I shared with Justin and Rob:

1) New learning, new insights, and new knowledge carry an energetic potential for change. The energetic potential is the "protein value" of learning.

2) At the point you receive and experience a new insight, the potency for change is 100%.

3) As the length of time increases from the exposure to the insight, the potential for change diminishes. Here is a way to look at this mathematically:
- The incidence of learning (the moment of impact)—100% potency for change
- Three hours lapse - 95%-98% potency
- 12 hours - 90% potency
- 24 hours - 85% potency
- 48 Hours - 75% potency
- 72 Hours - 51%-60% potency

4) Below 51%, the energetic potential for change is diluted to the point of ineffectuality.

5) The cycle of learning is about instantiating ideas and actualizing possibilities. When it works well, it becomes a virtuous spiral (*Portal Nine*) of growth and development. Here is what that cycle looks like: You
a) Receive: learn a new skill.
b) Understand: test the learning to validate and confirm it.
c) Apply: put the new skill to use within 72 hours.
d) Teach/own: success with the new skill motivates you to continue using the skill, teach it to others and learn more new skills.

6) The law of magnification holds that the virtuous spiral of learning builds its own momentum, as the energetic potential is magnified exponentially. By obtaining the first success with a new learned skill, the learning potency increases to 120%. By then teaching and modeling the new learning to someone else, the change potency increases to 150% and helps sustain the momentum of the learning application.

7) The leverage is in the velocity of implementation—how fast you move from idea to development and practice.

8) The compulsive hoarding of ideas and notes from a

workshop with no follow-up action is nothing more than intellectual gluttony. Unless you take action, the learning cycle becomes stuck, and the change potency quickly dissipates.

9) Sharing the new information or skill with others through teaching or coaching crystallizes your learning and enables you to achieve a new level of mastery.

10) An idea is only as good as its concretizing action. Move immediately to augment the potency of change and build the momentum of new results.

11) The "muscle" you need to practice is the concretizing muscle that determines your application velocity and accelerates the movement from idea up through the spiral to implementation.

Back to Rob and Justin. Rob was excited about the 22 learning ideas and key insights he had captured in copious notes. Justin directed his excitement to the three top ideas he had decided to implement immediately. His quick application of those insights generated significantly greater outcomes and momentum than Rob's focus on his notes of 22 attractive ideas. Implementation velocity trumps copious notes.

Takeoff Velocity

Justin's implementation velocity that stimulated the concept of the 72-hour rule and its related insights revitalized for me the connection between speed and learning. These insights proposed that learning opportunities come with a shelf life and, like other opportunity windows, they have expiration dates.

This experience made me think. Where else is momentum the defining factor? In what other fields have I seen that velocity is mission-critical?

The answer was there in front of me, in my own flying

experience. You cannot take off with a quarter or even half throttle. Momentum is the defining factor. Takeoff velocity is everything. Your runway is your takeoff window. You must develop enough velocity for takeoff before you reach the end of the runway.

Velocity creates lift. No velocity, no lift. If you use up the runway to accelerate and fail to reach the critical takeoff velocity, you crash at the end of the runway.

Practice application:

How do you build momentum to develop the necessary takeoff velocity to create the future of your organization? Here are five velocity engines I have observed in people who have mastered the takeoff dynamics:

1. **Clarity of focus**. Define clearly the problem you are working to solve.

2. **Simplicity**. Make the complex simple. Eliminate non-essential elements and features.

3. **Discipline**. Make inputs and protocol routine. Free up creative and innovating energy for well-defined opportunities.

4. **Agility**. Build adaptability and flexibility into the culture. Learn from agile systems. Encourage and demonstrate agility.

5. **Future prototype**. Build a prototype of the solution. Work from the desired future state backwards, and eliminate unnecessary steps.

Bring forward clarity, simplicity, discipline, agility, and a solution prototype to create takeoff velocity.

Lake Chapala, the Three Mindsets and Your Biggest Choice Ever

There are 30 Hewlett-Packard managers in the room. They have gathered from Argentina, Brazil, Chile, Columbia, and Mexico. We are meeting for four days in a resort near Lake Chapala, outside Guadalajara, Mexico. I have been helping this organization improve its business results and agility by building its leadership talent and energizing a culture of purposeful engagement.

To be a valuable catalyst to the future they intend to create, I must learn about their business and organizational vision, and internalize their professional and personal aspirations and hopes. They educate me about the Latin American cultures. The importance of family reminds me of the Israeli and Jewish family ethos. Their more relaxed way of looking at life is different, though. Then again, I am discovering that people all around the world are more alike than not. We all hope for and work for a better tomorrow.

How do I define work?

I have used the word work in the three-story house of work metaphor to mean and imply more than activity and effort. I propose we separate the idea of work from the notion of the dictionary synonyms: toil, slog, and drudgery. Instead, we embrace the mindset that work implies purpose, that it connotes creating value and producing benefit.

Many of us work to help others realize a better future, though our roles and process functions vary. Teaching, coaching, consulting, leading are each a process function that represents a distinctive set of modalities and behaviors. The unifying premise is that all of us seek to enable improved opportunities tomorrow. Ultimately, coaching, consulting, teaching, and leading are functions designed to facilitate new and better futures.

These thoughts fill me as I get up at 5 a.m. to prepare for the third morning of our leadership summit. I am searching for a way to introduce a new perspective that addresses a mindset that is holding the organization back from realizing its fullest transformative potential.

After our morning reflection ritual, in which people articulate their top takeaways from the previous day, I ask the group, "What are the three main religions in the world?"

This is the surprise method I discussed earlier. By asking a question people do not expect, we carve a new space for discovery and discussion. It works because I know exactly what I am after, and I use the question as a device to get me where I need to go with the group.

A ripple goes through the room because of the unwritten rule that you do not bring up religion in a corporate meeting. There are diverse cultural and religious backgrounds in the group, and the unwritten code of conduct is to leave religion outside of work.

After a moment of silence, someone volunteers an answer, "Christianity, Islam and Buddhism."

"Yes," I say, "and I am asking about the other three major religions. This is a reframing challenge, not a trick question."

Sensing their confusion, I offer, "While Christianity, Islam and Buddhism may be the three largest organized religions, what are the three major religions to which people pledge themselves? Reframe for a moment the meaning you attach to the word "religion." Think of it not as an institution, but as a mindset people embrace. What are the three mindsets that govern people's way of going on at work and in life, those that direct their response and engagement?"

Riddles work to sharpen people's thinking. I never use them casually, only as conversation portals with a specific intent. The managers try to resolve the riddle, and after using what they know and assume to be the case, they push their own thinking to explore new ideas. We go back and forth and work with answers offered by the group to surface the mental models that instruct their thinking.

To keep the search engaging, I use the hot/cold scale. "That's a good answer," I say to the first attempt. "It is a six and a half out of ten. How would you state an even broader case?" is a typical prompt I offer to keep the discovery going. And then, "You are really getting close; this probably gets us into the 9.3 zone; if you now can codify the essence of what you are saying, it will get us the answer."

At this point the entire group is engaged in the exercise, allowing me to bring forward the formulation I was seeking. The last 15 minutes produce sufficient energy to make the codified language potently memorable.

"There are three mindsets that I name as religions because people pledge allegiance to them in how they think, and because their tenets guide people's beliefs and behavior. They are the mindsets of 'what's wrong,' 'what works,' and 'what matters.'

"The first religion is the mindset of 'what's wrong.' This mindset is the most prevalent; it is the easiest of all and it gets the most air time. Ninety-five percent of what is presented every day as news is framed as fault, blame and wrong-doing. Unless you consciously make a different choice, finding 'what's wrong' is your default mindset, and you find yourself daily in the 'what's wrong' church.

"The second religion is the mindset of 'what works.' Although perhaps only five percent of the world's population consistently practice this mindset, thank God it often prevails. The world progresses by 'what works.' Choosing to follow the path of 'what works' and making it your template of response brings multiple blessings and energy. In the 'what works' temple, you empower yourself to participate in shaping and creating what can happen.

"The third religion and mindset builds upon the second and is the rarest of the three. This is the mindset of 'what matters.' All of us have the instinct of this mindset, but few act upon it to make 'what matters' our central, self-directed choice. For many people the impulse of 'what matters most' often is covered by the 'myth of tomorrow.' This is the myth that says, 'Tomorrow, next year, in five years, when I finish doing the things I have to do, I will be able to focus on what matters.

"These are the three major mindsets—the 'religions' people choose to practice: 'what's wrong,' 'what works' and 'what matters.' Every day you find yourself at this leadership crossroads where you are faced by these three. Your choice defines you as a leader."

I propose to the management team that this decision point is available for all of us in our lives and at work. You come to work and you can choose to focus on "what's wrong," or you can choose to focus on "what works," or on "what matters." The "what's wrong" preoccupation weakens you. The "what works" focus creates movement. And the "what matters" empowers and builds your impact and presence.

My description is followed by suspended silence. For a moment no one speaks. Many appear to be lost in deep reflection. We are touching something beyond the differences of our upbringing, a vein we all share. We all want to be involved in something that works, that matters and that makes a real difference.

The silence in the room is broken. "I have been in the 'what's wrong' religion far too long," says one manager. "I need to convert to the religion of 'what works.'"

Moving from "what's wrong" to "what works" is simple. It involves a pivotal and challenging decision. The conversion to "what works" is a shift from victimhood to personal responsibility. Choosing to take personal responsibility is the most pivotal decision you and I can make.

Indeed, the biggest choice we each can make is to let go of the preoccupation with "what's wrong" in favor of focusing on "what works."

The second conversion, from "what works" to "what matters," is the journey from success to significance.

Practice application:

Here are seven ways to apply the second and third mindsets and leave the first for those who cannot or will not make a different choice.

1. When you find yourself obsessing about what is wrong, pick yourself up and focus on something that works and that makes a difference. Develop an internal warning system that alerts you to shift your focus from problems to solutions.

2. Before pointing out what's wrong, point to two things that work. Even when you look at something that has failed, identify two or more of its elements that have worked.

3. Develop a weekly ritual of focusing on two or three things that matter.

4. Engage a coach to help you stay focused on what works and on what matters most to you.

5. Look at your team and organization and ask, "What's working well here? What matters most to us? What works for our employees, clients, and partners? What do we believe matters most to them?"

6. Develop an annual pilgrimage to the "what matters" oasis, where you can swim in the lake of significance and enjoy the sunshine of meaning, purpose, and true wealth.

7. Coach your team to focus on "what works" and "what matters." Make it an implicit shared experience. Discuss concrete examples. Become a leader of "what works" and "what matters."

Half Full and the Law of Magnification at Hair Masters

Chrystal has my reverence, as most hairdressers do, simply because she stands on her feet all day at work. She tells me that after work she relaxes by playing soccer. Even before I sit down, she begins the conversation. Clearly, Chrystal can teach me a lot about social skills. I don't need to ask her what is going on before she starts sharing. She is a master at making use of the captive audiences who sit in her chair. On this day I am called to offer her nothing less than the full measure of value in return.

Here is the conversation that transpired:

Chrystal: "My children visited with their father this week and came back today. I'm always glad to get them back."

Aviv: "It's good for children to see that adults can choose to go their separate ways without hating each other."

"I agree. I have to work hard at it. I want them to be able to tell me what they did with their father. I always worry about them."

This is the turning point in the conversation: should I get involved and bring new material into the dialogue, or not? Many conversations have this breaking open portal moment—a split second when you need to choose whether you will open and expose yourself or not. It is easier for me to listen to Chrystal than to bring myself into the conversation, but I decide to take the leap anyway.

"My parents separated when I was four. It was 51 years ago, and at that time divorce was quite rare where I grew up. By the age of six, I had decided that my situation was an advantage, rather than a predicament because I was able to benefit from both worlds."

"I wish my kids would have this attitude. But it is just so hard."

"Not really. At age seven, I realized that we always are making up a storyline for what is happening around us. It occurred to me that I could make up a half-empty or a half-full story. For me, the half-full story worked better."

"That's great. But most people don't see the world that way. For them, it is hard to see the full half because they see the empty half."

"Do you know why people prefer to focus on the empty half?" I asked.

"It's a lot easier to see it."

"Yes, Chrystal, the half-empty story provides an alibi. As long as you choose the half-empty story, you can keep the excuses that it affords you. People instinctively know that focusing on the half-full means giving up their excuses. We each have to choose: What do you love more, your excuses or your opportunities?

"That's a difficult choice."

"It's not. Look at you. You stand all day. That's difficult. I could not do it. It's actually easier to give up the excuses and take responsibility for the half-full perspective. You don't have to define yourself by your story of hardship. You can choose to form your identity on the basis of what you have been able to do and overcome."

"I wish we all could think like this, especially my children."

"Tell them that they can. Tell them you love them the way they are and that they don't need to hold on to half-empty stories to get more of you. Tell them they are better off loving the half-full world than the half-empty one. Tell them the secret of life is that whatever you focus on uses your energy to grow. It gets magnified with the attention you bring to it. When you focus on the half-empty, it continues to grow and you get a larger and larger empty. When you focus on your half-full, it grows and you get a larger and larger full."

"You made my day."

"You made my day, as well," I replied.

My haircut was done and I tipped Chrystal double because she helped me reclaim a lost childhood moment from my unconscious mind and triggered the half-full insight.

Epilogue

When to Pray

People pray most often when they need something. This is understandable; we most want health when it begins to fail, we desire friendship when we are lonely, and money becomes much more important when we don't have it.

But praying from a place of absence is not very effective. It is much better to pray for something within its presence. For example, when you feel most vital, pray to forward the gifts of vitality and strength you are experiencing to the future, for the days when you will need this strength to re-find you.

The best time to pray for fulfilling relationships is within their presence, when you are most appreciative of the richness you have. You ask for the ability to store the good memories so they may accompany you in days when you may feel lonely.

The best time to pray that you obtain clients is while you are serving a client, when you appreciate the opportunity to use your talent in service to others. The best time to pray for work opportunities that will improve your financial situation is when you enjoy your work and are feeling grateful for the opportunities presented to you.

The greatest prayer in the world is an act of kindness and generosity.

Abundance creates greater abundance.

Absence perpetuates want.

Presence grows presence.

The 39th Floor

"My name is John; I will be your waiter tonight. What can I get you started with?" He was bright and there was a happy melodic tone in his voice.

"John, it's a special evening. How about your favorite glass of red wine?" I replied.

I was sitting at the best table in the restaurant on the 39th floor of the Marriott in San Francisco. Something special had happened at the week's seminar, and I decided to relax and celebrate before taking the morning flight back home. For five days we had worked hard with a group of 12 executives. They each had a deep and meaningful experience during this seminar. All the executives had identified their strengths, articulated their core values, envisioned the roadmap ahead, and aligned their short-term goals with their long-term aims.

The advisory brief I offer is that you work on the long-term by taking concrete steps toward these long-term aims in the short-term. Similarly, as you work on your near-term goals, keeping the long-term in mind fuels your efforts with sustainable energy. Without pragmatic action in the here and now, the long-term remains a dream. You leave yourself unnecessarily vulnerable if you work on today without a long-term compass.

The fact that each person had undergone a breakthrough moment made the week's work an enriching experience. Now that the seminar was over, it was my time to reflect and treat myself. Deciding to enjoy a special dinner, I reserved the nicest table available with a view of the city. Sunsets in San Francisco can be very beautiful, and the one that night matched my contemplative mood.

John was back with his favorite glass of wine in minutes. I selected the finest dish on the menu and we started talking. He inquired about the occasion and I explained the nature of the work we had just completed.

John commented astutely, "It must feel good to know you have done your best and that your efforts have made a difference, that your work impacts people's lives positively."

"Yes, very much so, John. For a few days we were able to focus on what matters and take a broader view of our lives. The participants are tough, 24/7, pedal-to-the-metal executives. By allowing themselves to enter a different portal and engage in conversations about purpose, they were able to find a great sense of renewal," I explained. "We were able to push back pressures and find the convergence zone, where the personal and the professional are in alignment. They each found a point where the various roles they play in life are expressions of a central principle—their purpose. Each experienced a Michelangelo moment."

"The Michelangelo moment, sounds awesome," said John, with a smile and a curious look in his eyes.

The sculpture of David is recognized as one of the greatest works of art in the world. Its creator, Michelangelo, is reported to have said that David already was inside the rock; all he had to do was chisel away that which was not David.

A "Michelangelo moment" occurs when you recognize your own "David in the rock"—when you discover that your greater potential arises from your essence, when the focus shifts from acquiring more outside "things" to seeing and appreciating your purpose on the inside, and beginning to chisel away everything that is not your essence.

A Michelangelo moment is the realization that your essence already is here, inside you, and that your work is to carve away and discard whatever hides it so you can discover and express the motivating force of your life. Your life's experiences—the triumph and the setbacks, the ups and the downs—all offer you opportunities to refine the great work of art that is you.

Although sharing these thoughts with my waiter would be out of place in many situations, I sensed in John an innate intelligence, so I did not censor the extemporaneous flow of the conversation. It turned out that John was a bit of a philosopher, or at least he had done a lot of thinking about what matters to him. As the evening progressed he stopped by periodically and our conversation evolved further. I watched him work his tables. He had a spring in his step as he approached each one with great sensitivity and attunement.

"John," I asked, as he brought the dessert menu, "why are you working here? You clearly have a lot going on in you. What is your real passion?"

John smiled and said, "I am a poet. In the morning I get up and write poems. That is where my passion is, but it doesn't pay the bills. I need a money-making job to support what I love to do. Working here during the evening shift is a great way to pay the bills. I meet interesting people and I try to make them feel special. It's a bit like writing a poem. Some nights I get to meet families on their special happy occasions; other nights I see a successful businessman who has everything and is sad and lonely. I try to fit my style and approach to rhyme with the person at the table I serve. Every person deserves to have a good dinner. Plus, it stimulates my creativity and gives me ideas for my poems."

He came back with a rich chocolate cake, a fitting completion to the evening. Looking at the check, I could not recall ever spending that amount of money on a solo dinner for myself. At that time, I was in the early stages of my consulting business, so this was not an insignificant sum for me. However, it was an evening to celebrate abundance and appreciate the wellbeing that accompanies a job well done. I doubled the check and rounded the numbers up again to leave a large tip with a little card for John, "Thank you. This is for your poems. Keep up the good work. Blessings...."

Your Accelerating Universe

The premise of this book has centered on the belief that each of us has the power to create new futures.

Awarding the 2011 Nobel Prize in physics to Saul Perlmutter, Adam Riess, and Brian Schmidt for discovering the acceleration of the expansion of the universe inspired a whole new kind of realization about life, and empowered us to explore the breakthrough implications of their work.

Thomas Kuhn, who popularized the term "paradigm shift," observes in his controversial book *The Structure of Scientific Revolutions* that scientific progress does not follow a continuous linear trajectory. Rather, he makes an argument for a disruptive and episodic model in which a period of conceptual continuity is interrupted by a period of revolutionary science.

From the beginning of time, humans have struggled to embrace new paradigms about the world and about themselves. We now are living through a dramatically disruptive period where breakdowns and breakthroughs converge into confusing and chaotic change. Problems seem impossibly intractable in Washington, in Europe, in the Middle East, in Asian geopolitics, and in the global financial system. Yet amidst the dysfunction and impossibility, profound breakthroughs, system upgrades, and portals of possibility are available right here, right now, when leaders embrace the paradigm of an accelerating universe.

Man's view of the universe is a reflection of man's view of himself. As toddlers, we see ourselves as the center of the world. As most of us grow up, we are surprised to discover that the world does not revolve around us. Some, however, remain frozen at the toddler's pre-Copernican age and view of the world.

Until Copernicus developed his heliocentric model with the sun at its center, the general perception put the Earth at the center of the universe. When Galileo improved the telescope and observed Jupiter and the Milky Way, he described celestial movements that were contrary to church doctrines and hinted at an even bigger universe. He was tried by the Inquisition, found "vehemently suspect of heresy" and spent the rest of his life under house arrest. Luckily, discovering a new scientific paradigm today is not likely to land you in house arrest, although you should not be surprised to face a mountain of resistance and derision at first.

However, we face an even greater risk today. By refusing to embrace a new map of the world, we hold ourselves back, effectively putting ourselves under house arrest. Accepting and embracing a new paradigm changes our view of the world and of ourselves.

In 1922, using the best telescope of his time, Edwin Hubble observed the Andromeda Nebula. He realized it was much too distant to be part of the Milky Way and was, in fact, an entire galaxy outside our own. Hubble's findings fundamentally changed the scientific view of the universe, which expanded beyond the Milky Way galaxy.

The Big Bang theory was proposed in 1927, though it did not get its name until 22 years later. In 1929, the year of the big market crash which ushered in the Great Depression, Hubble observed that the distance between galaxy clusters was increasing. Not only was the universe bigger than our local galaxy, it was expanding as a consequence of the Big Bang some 14 billion years earlier. For several decades, the reigning paradigm was that the universe had expanded before it began to slow down. Leading thinkers believed the universe was forced to decelerate as it cooled down from its initial heated explosion. When scientists set out to measure the rate of deceleration, they were stunned. In 1998, scientists Saul Perlmutter, Brian Schmidt and Adam Riess led teams that discovered, to their amazement and horror, that rather than decelerating, the universe's expansion was accelerating. This discovery shattered the foundations of cosmology and physics yet again, and earned the three scientists the 2011 Nobel Prize in physics.

Acceleration of the universe's expansion means it is pumping out extra space between celestial bodies at a faster rate than before. Imagine looking out your window and seeing the houses around yours moving farther and farther away at an accelerating speed. That's what is happening to celestial bodies and galaxies when they "look" at each other through their windows. They are being pushed farther and farther apart at a faster and faster rate. This discovery was astounding, and required scientists to rethink their models yet again. The shift to a universe that accelerates its expansion required the same rethinking of everything that the shift from a geocentric to a heliocentric system required. The discovery produced a new set of questions: What is causing this acceleration? What is the universe expanding into? What will happen as expansion continues to speed up?

Scientists now believe the acceleration is caused by dark energy. Astronomers have mapped a record-breaking 1.2 million galaxies to study the properties of dark energy. But no one knows what this dark energy is or what causes it. Mathematical formulas suggest that dark energy constitutes about three-quarters of the universe. If true, we are only scratching the surface of understanding the nature and make-up of the universe. For all we know, dark energy could be contained in another invisible dimension or series of dimensions, a universe within a universe, or a series of universes invisibly hiding inside each other like the Russian Babushka dolls.

Your Universe: As Above, So Below

How do these discoveries into the nature of the universe impact our self-understanding?

The adage "As above, so below" has served through the ages as a thread of discovery. It proposes that "man is made in the image of God." This represents a discovery brief rather than a metaphor or theological concept. The "as above, so below" creed intimates that learning about the universe offers a theater of revelation about us humans, and equally, that the study of human life contains potent revelations for the study of the stars. These ideas inspire the realization that atomic structures are replicas of systems like our own solar system, that the cellular structure emulates the formation of galaxies, and that the three-dimensional pictures that map distant galaxies look much the same as similar maps of the brain's neural structure. The cosmic and the microscopic reflect and reveal each other; together they propel us to pursue scientific discovery and to birth creative expression in art.

Nonlinear discoveries in the space surrounding us help us recognize that we, too, are nonlinear. Spontaneous phenomena in the natural worlds inspire us to be extemporaneous in our music, in our dance and in our conversations.

How are we different because of the game-changing discovery that the universe is accelerating? What are we to make of ourselves if the universe is pumping out extra energy and space between celestial bodies at an accelerated rate?

If you and I are a mirror reflection of the cosmos, what are we to make of the discovery that the universe contains immense amounts of invisible energy potential?

How would we view ourselves and our creative possibilities if we embraced the idea that, like the universe at large, all humans contain huge amounts of unrealized and latent energy and creative potential?

Imagine that you, too, are a universe within a universe, where, as is the case of the cosmos, three-quarters of your potential is invisible and unrealized. I know, it is a little hard to wrap your mind around this idea. Here is a way to begin to explore and come inside this paradigm shift and portal into a new future.

Pulled by Tomorrow

Every few years along your journey from childhood to adulthood, and then through your professional career, you get to a point where one day you look around and the world seems different. Your view of it has changed, like it did on your first day of high school, or the first time you left home, or when you got your first job, or when you became a parent.

Other, more subtle changes occur when your perspective simply shifts on its own, without being triggered by external events. You wonder whether something around you is different, or whether you have changed when suddenly you are able to see what was always there in front of you, yet revealed itself only now.

Consider this universe-changing discovery. We know that the universe accelerates by some invisible dark energy that we are not yet able to detect or pinpoint. The implication is that it is moving toward its future state at an increasingly faster rate.

How can you and I internalize this idea? How can we accelerate toward our own future? In what ways can we live an accelerating universe-like life? What would our lives look like?

Though it sounds wacky, come along with me for this mind-bending thought experiment. Imagine a life in which the gravitational pull of tomorrow is greater than that of yesterday. You get up in the morning and define yourself more strongly by what you are becoming today and next month than by who and what you were last year. Do you realize the transformative power of living into your future, free of the gravitational pull of your past?

Every major breakthrough in thought was propelled by people who were pulled forward to live into the future. Similarly, major breakthroughs in science, as well as innovations in technology, medicine, design, art, and other fields, were led by people who leaned into the future by harnessing the power of an accelerating universe.

The world and our experience in it were accelerated significantly with the development of the Internet. Curiously, the 1998 discovery of the accelerating universe coincided with its advent. We were learning to tap the invisible power of cyberspace at the same time that we discovered the universe was filled with invisible "dark energy." Here again, our experience was a mirror image of our view of the universe.

Become a Universe-like Person

Imagine this invisible energy is agenda-free. It can be released into creativity or destruction. The destructive and creative cycles are intertwined. Rapid technological innovation created new businesses and quickly destroyed others. New modes of communication enabled innovative social networking phenomena that empowered emergent movements throughout the globe and disrupted powerful regimes. These examples represent the nature of an accelerating universe—it seems to appear from nowhere, then quickly gathers energy and momentum to surprise us.

What about you? What invisible energy powers you? What is the gravitational pull that drives your world?

Your universe accelerates when you prioritize action over perfection. It accelerates when you forgive quickly. It leaps forward when you live into today, free of the opinions of others. It picks up speed again when you dare to imagine what can be, and when you act on your beliefs with conviction.

Our universe can accelerate in ways that surprise us. Here are a few examples of what becomes possible as you practice living into that future every day:

- Transformation: You have the power to transform your life by releasing old habits instantly.
- Forgiveness: You can choose to forgive yourself and others instantly, which accelerates your endeavors.
- Problem solving: We all have the capacity to solve intractable, complex problems. This requires that, like the accelerating universe, the power that propels you to a future state becomes greater by an order of magnitude than the power that compels the old or ancient state.
- Collaboration: We dramatically accelerate the journey from ideation to the creation of results that produce value and meaning when we work collaboratively with others.
- Growing young: This paradigm shift is somewhat more difficult to grasp. Imagine that while you grow old, another

part of you is growing young. Living into an accelerated future means you are growing young, not in chronological terms, but in how your potential and ability to create an impact continues to grow exponentially. Meditate on this for a day to begin to discover how this opens up your creative and leadership potential.

We All Were Impostors Once

"I feel like an impostor," Jane told me. She was one of the brightest young professionals I had ever encountered, much wiser than her young age might lead you to think. "Sometimes I am amazed at the responsibilities and opportunities handed to me. Inside of me is a nagging fear that I may be found out, that I cannot be that good," she added.

The other names for the impostor anxiety are the "fear of becoming an authority" or "the fear of having power." Many people suffer from and grapple with a form of this anxiety. I, too, have experienced my share.

I skipped the academic route, and I largely skipped the corporate road. Instead, I chose to travel a different path. In my mid-forties, my father-in-law continued to ask occasionally when I would start studying at the university. "But Moshe," I would smile, "do you realize I already have PhDs and senior executives participating in my seminars, coming to learn from me?" Like my father, his educational opportunity was stolen during World War II, when he escaped Warsaw to join the Jewish Brigade in the Russian Army to fight in support of the Allied forces. For the rest of his life, he retained his desire and love for education.

I am lucky. Both my father and mother learned early on to trust that I was following my own inner guidance. In fairness, they each struggled with their own full plates of responsibilities, leaving me largely to my own devices and convictions. A true gift indeed.

I realized Jane was asking me to afford her the same

validation I had received from my parents. "How can I provide the touch of confidence and self-belief she needs?" was the question I pondered. I sat down to write the following letter to Jane.

Dear Jane,

When it comes to overcoming fear and anxiety, consider that you already have conquered the first great fear that every human must face: that of appearing in this world. Nothing can be more overwhelming than being born into this strange world. The sheer courage to emerge from the womb into the helplessness of total dependence on the adults around you (who in some cases are ill-informed and not very helpful) is powerful beyond compare.

Some will say the reality of being born is inescapable and automatic. However, I believe it represents the greatest act of courage and faith, more significant by an order of magnitude than any other we perform thereafter. The awesome realization that a soul presence and a spirit inhabit the body early in its development to fortify the birthing act, signifies for me the great light that shines through every day of my earthly living.

When I am beset with fears, I remind myself of the courage of my birth. I then recall the incredible challenges I have overcome, and the miraculous events that followed as a result. I remember the heart specialist who never looked me in the eye when he said to my father, "Your son has a condition that needs to be monitored and he should not exert himself," which I mistakenly interpreted as a death sentence. Talk about fear... I was left physically shaking. To banish that fear I started running in earnest, winning the Israeli long distance running championship five years later. None of my competitors knew that I was not competing with them, but fighting against my own fear.

Later, as an Air Force pilot, I nearly crashed more than once and had a few flight near-misses. Those experiences made me realize that I never am alone, never without support or guidance. Even when I fall on my face, I am not without help, except in times when I allow fear to separate me from the bounty of care and guidance that is freely offered. And even then, I still am being watched over in spite of myself. We all are. There is evidence galore that so much in this universe is willing and ready to help you, to help me, to help us all. Much is invested in our success. My improbable journey and yours bear testimony to this truth.

Living is a theater. We all are here on a journey of discovery. Pretending or faking it until it is real is one of the fastest ways to syphon learning. We all were impostors on the first day of school, the first time on the soccer field or in the choir, the first time we were caught up in the act of love, and in the first solo attempt at driving. Impostor anxiety is merely the echoing hangover of these experiences.

Therefore, central to the development journey is the updating of one's own self-view. As we grow, we all must release the old self-views that no longer serve us well.

Living is about overcoming setbacks, disappointments and challenges. It is a journey in which you make new connections, unfolding the reason and purpose why you are here on this Earth at this time, and get closer to the supreme realization and knowing that your life matters.

The vistas of possibilities that have opened up in my life extend beyond what I had imagined. More often than not, they have been a source of great surprises. The most radical moments of breakthrough always found me when I was able to gently unburden myself of my limiting beliefs. Often these beliefs centered on a view I had held dearly and could not imagine being without. Time and again, a methodology or a way of working that had seemed essential, with no apparent way to proceed without it, would then appear to be a figment of my own imagination that had initially acted as my crutches. All I had to do was lay them down and release the mental model that had enabled them in the first place.

There is very little we achieve or do on our own. I would not be where I am today without the help of many people. I never forget this fact. There has been a chain of never-ending miracle workers: the teacher who did not give up on me when I struggled, the stranger who rescued me at a point of desperate need, the friends and communities that still provide me with fortitude, the clients who trusted me. The list goes on.

I tell you this for a fact: as you wake up every day, many people—some knowingly, but many not—are conspiring to help you take the next step to carry you forward, to help you grow and evolve beyond your wildest imagination.

Always remember, there is an army of helpers fighting for you, even when you do not see them. They need you to do your part. They need you to make an effort. They need you to make your next move in order for them to show up and help. And you, too, are part of an army of helpers for others, some of whom you know, others whom you do not.

You are here for a purpose. Remember, you have an extraordinary gift. You can learn today what you did not know yesterday. Time and again I have been in situations that felt like I was drinking from a fire hose. Without exception, the learning journey is non-linear. Learning even can bend time. When the need is urgent, certain interventions can be designed to create an immediate transfer of three months' worth of learning in just three days, or even faster.